MISSISSIPPI RULES OF CRIMINAL PROCEDURE

© 2021 Mississippi Legal Publishing, LLC
No part of this edition of the Mississippi Rules of Criminal Procedure may be sold, commercially distributed, or used for any other commercial purpose without the written permission of Mississippi Legal Publishing. No copyright claim is made as to government works.

ISBN: 9798727316580

Peter Edwards, Esq.
Mississippi Legal Publishing, LLC

MISSISSIPPI RULES OF CRIMINAL PROCEDURE

Rule 1   General Provisions

Rule 2   Commencement of Criminal Proceedings

Rule 3   Arrest Warrant or Summons upon Commencement of Criminal Proceedings

Rule 4   Search Warrants

Rule 5   Arrest and Initial Appearance

Rule 6   Preliminary Hearing

Rule 7   Counsel

Rule 8   Release

Rule 9   Trial Setting

Rule 10   Presence of Defendant, Witnesses, and Spectators

Rule 11   Change of the Place of Trial

Rule 12   Mental Examinations

Rule 13   The Grand Jury

Rule 14   Indictment

Rule 15   Arraignment and Pleas

Rule 16   Pre-Trial Motions

Rule 17   Disclosure and Discovery

Rule 18   Trial by Jury; Waiver; Selection and Preparation of Petit Jury; Prohibited Disclosures

Rule 19   Trial

Rule 20   Duties of Court Reporters

Rule 21   Motions for Directed Verdict

Rule 22   Jury Instructions

Rule 23   Deliberations

Rule 24   Verdict

Rule 25   Post-Trial Motions

Rule 26   Judgment

Rule 27   Probation

Rule 28   Retention of Records and Evidence

Rule 29   Appeals from Justice or Municipal Court

Rule 30   Appeals from County Court

Rule 31   Post-Conviction Collateral Relief

Rule 32   Contempt

Rule 33   Subpoenas

Rule 34   Motions

MISSISSIPPI RULES OF CRIMINAL PROCEDURE

Rule 1 General Provisions

Rule 1.1 Scope.
These are the Mississippi Rules of Criminal Procedure and shall govern the procedure in all criminal proceedings, from arrest through post-trial motions, in all trial courts within the State of Mississippi, except as otherwise provided in these Rules. They may be cited as MRCrP; e.g., MRCrP 1.

Comment
The Mississippi Rules of Criminal Procedure are designed to provide comprehensive and uniform practice and procedure for criminal proceedings in all Mississippi trial courts, including justice courts, municipal courts, county courts, and circuit courts, except as otherwise provided. They replace practice under formerly applicable provisions of the Uniform Rules of Circuit and County Court and the Uniform Rules of Procedure for Justice Court.

"It is now well established that 'the constitutional concept of separation of powers dictates that it is within the inherent power of this Court to promulgate procedural rules to govern judicial matters.' Thus, when a statute conflicts with this Court's rules regarding matters of judicial procedure, our rules control." **State v. Delaney**, 52 So. 3d 348, 351 (Miss. 2011) (internal citations omitted).

Rule 1.2 Purpose and Construction.
These Rules are to be interpreted to provide for the just and speedy determination of criminal proceedings, to secure simplicity in procedure and fairness in administration, to eliminate unjustifiable delay and expense, and to protect the rights of individuals while protecting the public.

Rule 1.3 Computation and Enlargement of Time.
(a) Computation. In computing any period of time prescribed or allowed by these Rules, by order of court, or by any applicable statute, the day of the act, event, or default from which the designated period of time begins to run shall

not be included. The last day of the period so computed shall be included, unless it is a Saturday, a Sunday, or a legal holiday, as defined by statute, or any other day when the court clerk's office is in fact closed, whether with or without legal authority, in which event the period runs until the end of the next day which is not a Saturday, a Sunday, a legal holiday, or any other day when the court clerk's office is in fact closed. In the event any legal holiday falls on a Sunday, the next day shall be a legal holiday. When the period of time prescribed or allowed is less than seven (7) days, intermediate Saturdays, Sundays, and legal holidays shall be excluded in the computation.

(b) Enlargement. When by these Rules or by order of court an act is required or allowed to be done at or within a specified time, the court may at any time:

> (1) with or without motion, and for cause shown, order the period enlarged if request therefor is made before the expiration of the period originally prescribed or as extended by a previous order; or

> (2) upon motion made after the expiration of the specified period, permit the act to be done where failure to act was the result of excusable neglect or good cause shown.

But a court may not, except as provided elsewhere in these Rules, extend the time for making a motion for directed verdict, a motion for new trial, a motion to vacate judgment, or for taking an appeal.

(c) Unaffected by Expiration of Term. The doing of any act or the taking of any action permitted by these Rules is not affected or limited by the existence or expiration of a term of court. However, a criminal sentence cannot be modified, altered, or vacated after the end of the term of court in which the defendant was sentenced, except as provided by law.

(d) Motions Regarding Computation and Enlargement of Time. A written motion, other than one which may be heard *ex parte*, and notice of the hearing thereof, shall be served not later than five (5) days before the time fixed for the hearing, unless a different period is fixed by these Rules or by order of the court.

Such an order may, for cause shown, be made on *ex parte* application. Service shall be accomplished in accordance with Rule 1.7.

(e) Additional Time After Service by Mail. Whenever a party has the right or is required to do some act or take some action within a prescribed period after the service of a notice or other paper and the notice or paper is served by mail, three (3) days shall be added to the prescribed period.

Comment

Rule 1.3 is derived from Rule 6 of the Mississippi Rules of Civil Procedure.

Section (b) provides the court with wide discretion to enlarge various time periods both before and after the actual termination of the allotted time, with the notable exceptions of motions for directed verdict (Rule 21), motions for new trial (Rule 25.1), motions to vacate judgment (Rule 25.2), or appeals (Rules 29 and 30). Importantly, such enlargement is to be made only for cause shown. If the application for additional time is made before the period expires, the request may be made *ex parte*; if it is made after the expiration of the period, notice of the motion shall be given to other parties and the only cause for which extra time can be allowed is "excusable neglect or good cause shown."

Section (c) does not abolish court terms. This Rule merely provides greater flexibility to the courts in attending the myriad functions they must perform, many of which were previously possible only during term time. The Rule is also consistent with provisions elsewhere herein that prescribe a specific number of days for taking certain actions rather than linking time expirations to the opening day, final day, or any other day of a term of court. The rule recognizes that judges do not have the authority to modify, alter, or vacate a criminal sentence after the end of the term of court during which the sentence was given, except as otherwise provided by law. *See **Creel v. State**, 944 So. 2d 891 (Miss. 2006); **Miss. Comm'n of Jud. Performance v. Russell**, 691 So. 2d 929 (Miss. 1997).

Rule 1.4 Definitions.

Unless otherwise defined in a particular Rule, whenever they appear in these Rules, the terms below shall have the following meanings:

(a) "Bill of information" means a written statement charging the defendant(s) named therein with the commission of an indictable offense, made on oath, signed, and presented to the court by the district attorney, without action by the grand jury.

(b) "Capias" means a writ commanding law enforcement officers to take into custody a defendant for whom a grand jury has returned an indictment.

(c) "Charge" means a charging affidavit, indictment, or bill of information.

(d) "Charging affidavit" means a written statement made upon oath before a judge, clerk of the court, or other officer authorized by law to administer oaths, setting forth essential underlying facts and circumstances constituting an offense and alleging that the defendant committed the offense.

(e) "Indictment" is a written statement charging the defendant(s) named therein with the commission of an indictable offense, presented to the court by a grand jury, endorsed "A True Bill," and signed by the foreperson. It includes a true bill from the grand jury or a bill of information in lieu thereof.

(f) "Offense" means conduct for which a fine, a sentence to a term of imprisonment, or the death penalty may be imposed pursuant to any law of this State or by any law or ordinance of a political subdivision of this State.

(g) "*Pro se*" means a party who represents himself or herself and is not represented by an attorney.

(h) "Prosecuting Attorney" means any municipal or county attorney, district attorney, attorney general, or other attorney(s) acting under their specific direction and authority, or such other person appointed or charged by law with the responsibility for prosecuting an offense.

(i) "Search warrant" means a written order based upon a finding of probable cause, in the name of the State, county, or municipality, signed by a judge authorized by law to issue search warrants, directed to any authorized law enforcement officer, commanding the officer to search for and seize a person and/or thing.

(j) "Sentencing Court" includes the court which imposes the sentence and any court to which jurisdiction has been transferred.

(k) "Summons" means a written order notifying an individual that he or she has been charged with an offense and directing the individual to appear in court to answer the charge.

Rule 1.5 Information on Each Pleading and Motion.
(a) Pleadings filed by counsel. All pleadings, motions, or other applications to the court shall bear the name, address, bar association number, email address, and office phone number of the attorney who will try the case and, if different from the attorney who will try the case, the name, address, bar association number, email address, and office phone number of the attorney who will be prepared to argue the pleading, motion or other application.

(b) Pleadings filed *pro se*. All pleadings, motions, or other applications to the court shall bear the name, address, email address, and phone number of the party proceeding *pro se*.

Comment
Rule 1.5(a) continues practice under former Rule 1.05 of the Uniform Rules of Circuit and County Court. Rule 1.5(b) addresses *pro se* pleadings. *See* Miss. Const. art. 3, § 26 ("[i]n all criminal prosecutions the accused shall have a right to be heard by himself or counsel, or both").

Rule 1.6 Size of Paper.
All papers filed in any proceeding governed by these Rules shall be on paper measuring eight and one-half (8½) inches by eleven (11) inches. Notwithstanding the foregoing, exhibits or attachments to pleadings may be

folded and fastened to pages of the specified size. An exhibit or attachment not in compliance with the foregoing provisions may be filed only if it appears that compliance is not reasonably practicable.

Rule 1.7 Service and Filing of Pleadings and Certificate of Service.
(a) Service: When Required. Unless otherwise ordered by the court, any person filing a pleading, motion, or application to the court, except the initial pleading or an indictment, shall:

> (1) serve a correct copy of that pleading, motion, or application to the court on all attorneys of record in the case, and any unrepresented defendant, pursuant to section (b) of this rule; and

> (2) file with the court an original certificate of service certifying that a correct copy of the pleading, motion, or application to the court has been served on all attorneys of record in the case, and on any unrepresented defendant, pursuant to section (b) of this rule; stating the manner of service; and identifying on whom it was served.

(b) Service How Made
(1) Generally. Whenever under these Rules service is required or permitted to be made upon a party who is represented by an attorney of record in the proceedings, the service shall be made upon such attorney unless service upon the party is ordered by the court. Service upon the attorney or upon a party shall be made by:

> (A) personally handing a copy to the attorney/party;

> (B) transmitting it to the attorney/party by electronic means; or

> (C) mailing it to the attorney/party at the last known address.

Service by electronic means is complete when the electronic equipment being used by the attorney or party being served acknowledges receipt of the material.

If the equipment used by the attorney or party being served does not automatically acknowledge the transmission, service is not complete until the sending party obtains an acknowledgment from the recipient. Service by mail is complete upon mailing.

(2) Electronic Court System Service. Where a court has, by local rule, adopted the Mississippi Electronic Court System, service which is required or permitted under these Rules shall be made in conformity with the Mississippi Electronic Court System procedures.

(c) Filing With the Court Defined.

(1) Generally. The filing of pleadings and other papers with the court as required by these Rules shall be made by filing them with the clerk of the court, except that the judge may permit the papers to be filed with the judge, in which event the judge shall note thereon the filing date and forthwith transmit them to the office of the clerk.

(2) Electronic Filing. A court may, by local rule, allow pleadings and other papers to be filed, signed, or verified by electronic means in conformity with the Mississippi Electronic Court System procedures. Pleadings and other papers filed electronically in compliance with the procedures are written papers for purposes of these Rules.

Comment

Rule 1.7(a) carries forward applicable provisions of former Rule 2.06 of the Uniform Rules of Circuit and County Court. Sections (b) and (c) track provisions in Rule 5(b) and (e) of the Mississippi Rules of Civil Procedure.

Rule 1.8 Interactive Audiovisual Devices.

(a) General Provisions. When the appearance of a defendant or counsel is required in circuit, county, municipal or justice court, subject to the provisions of this Rule, the appearance may be made by the use of interactive audiovisual equipment, including video conferencing equipment. Interactive audiovisual equipment shall at a minimum operate so as to enable the court and all parties to view and converse with each other.

(b) Requirements. In using interactive audiovisual equipment, the following are required:

> (1) a full record of the proceedings shall be made as provided in applicable rules;

> (2) the court shall determine that the defendant knowingly, intelligently, and voluntarily agrees to appear at the proceeding by interactive audiovisual means; and

> (3) provisions shall be made to allow for confidential communications between the defendant and counsel before and during the proceeding. Defense counsel shall be present at the location with the defendant during the proceedings.

(c) Permissible Proceedings. Appearance by interactive audiovisual equipment, including video conferencing, may be permitted in the discretion of the court at any proceeding except that this Rule shall not apply to any trial, probation violation hearing, or any felony plea and/or sentencing.

Comment

Section (a) is taken from former Rule 6.08 of the Uniform Rules of Circuit and County Court. Section (b) preserves a defendant's right to be present personally under Rule 10.1(a), by providing that a defendant must consent to appear by interactive audiovisual means. While section (c) generally puts the use of such technology in the discretion of the court, Rule 1.8 is inapplicable to trials, probation violation hearings, and felony pleas and sentencing.

Rule 1.9 Local Court Rules.

(a) When Permissible. Any court by action of a majority of the judges thereof may hereafter make local rules and amendments thereto concerning practice in their respective courts not inconsistent with these Rules. In the event there is no majority, the senior judge shall have an additional vote.

(b) Procedure for Approval. All such local rules shall be submitted to the Supreme Court of Mississippi for approval before taking effect. Such submissions shall comply with the requirements of Rule 27(f) of the Mississippi Rules of Appellate Procedure and should include the text of the proposed new rule or of the rule to be amended with deletions indicated by strikeouts and additions shown underlined. The submissions shall also be accompanied by a copy of the motion and of the proposed rule or rule amendment in an electronically formatted medium (such as a USB Flash Drive or CD-ROM). Upon receipt of such proposed rules and before any approval of the same, the Supreme Court may submit them to the Supreme Court Advisory Committee on Rules for advice as to whether any such rules are consistent or in conflict with these Rules or any other rules adopted by the Supreme Court.

(c) Publication. All local rules hereinafter approved by the Supreme Court shall be submitted for publication on the Court's website, in the Southern Reporter (Mississippi cases), and in the Mississippi Rules of Court.

Comment

Rule 1.9 largely tracks Rule 83 of the Mississippi Rules of Civil Procedure. Rule 1.9 guarantees the right of trial judges to prescribe local rules of court, not inconsistent with these Rules. Consistent with Rule 27(f) of the Mississippi Rules of Appellate Procedure, all local rules shall be filed in motion form with the Supreme Court of Mississippi and are not effective until approved by the Supreme Court.

Rule 1.10 Recordation of Proceedings where Official Court Reporter not Provided.

Any attorney of record or *pro se* litigant in a court which does not provide an official court reporter may record or have recorded any court proceeding by audio-recording device or stenographically. Any expenses incident thereto shall be borne by the party or parties.

Comment

Rule 1.10 is consistent with current practice and Mississippi Code Section 9-13-32.

Rule 2 Commencement of Criminal Proceedings

Rule 2.1 Commencement of Criminal Proceedings.
(a) Commencement. All criminal proceedings shall be commenced either by charging affidavit, indictment, or bill of information.

(b) Docketing the Case.
(1) Charging affidavit. Anyone bringing a criminal charge in municipal court or justice court shall lodge a charging affidavit with the judge or clerk of the court. The clerk of the court shall record all charging affidavits on the docket.

(2) Indictment. After the grand jury returns an indictment, the circuit clerk shall mark the indictment "filed" and such entries shall be dated and signed by the circuit clerk. The circuit clerk shall, within ten (10) days after adjournment of the term of court, record the indictments in the "Secret Record of Indictments," which shall be indexed and kept secret. The circuit clerk shall issue a capias to the sheriff of the county where the indictment was returned. A copy of the indictment shall be attached to the capias. Upon the execution of the capias and the officer's return thereon, the case shall be assigned a cause number in the criminal docket and this cause number shall be put on the capias instanter.

Comment

Under Rule 2.1(a), the procedure for commencing a criminal proceeding is either by charging affidavit or by indictment. By definition, "indictment" includes "a bill of information in lieu thereof." *See* Rule 1.4(e). This is in accord with article 3, section 27, of the Mississippi Constitution of 1890, and consistent with Mississippi Code Section 99-1-7.

The procedures for docketing the case provided in (b) are consistent with Mississippi Code Sections 9-7-175, 99-7-9, 99-7-13, 99-9-1, and 99-33-2. Additional rules regarding the grand jury are found in Rule 13, and rules regarding indictments are found in Rule 14.

Rule 2.2 Duty of Judge upon Making of a Charging Affidavit.

(a) Probable Cause Determination. If it appears from the charging affidavit and the evidence submitted that there is probable cause to believe that the offense complained of has been committed and that there is probable cause to believe that the defendant committed it, the judge shall proceed under Rule 3.1. Before ruling on a request for a warrant, the judge may examine under oath the affiant and any witnesses the affiant may produce.

(b) Evidence. The finding of probable cause shall be based upon evidence, which may be hearsay in whole or in part provided there is a basis for believing the source of the hearsay to be credible and for believing that there is a factual basis for the information furnished.

Comment

The purposes served by Rule 2.2 are in accord with Mississippi law and the mandates of the Fourth Amendment to the United States Constitution. As the United States Supreme Court stated in *Giordenello v. United States*, 357 U.S. 480, 78 S. Ct. 1245, 2 L. Ed. 2d 1503 (1958):

> [t]he purpose of the [charging affidavit], then, is to enable the [judge] . . . to determine whether the "probable cause" required to support a warrant exists. The [judge] must judge for himself the persuasiveness of the facts relied on by a[n] [affiant] to show probable cause. [The judge] should not accept without question the [affiant's] mere conclusion that the person whose arrest is sought has committed a crime.

Id. at 486. *See also* Miss. Code Ann. § 99-3-28 (regarding "[w]arrants against teachers, jail officers or counselors at adolescent offender programs"); *State v. Delaney*, 52 So. 3d 348 (Miss. 2011).

Rule 3 Arrest Warrant or Summons upon Commencement of Criminal Proceedings

Rule 3.1 Issuance of Arrest Warrant or Summons.

(a) Issuance. Upon a finding of probable cause made pursuant to Rule 2.2, or upon a finding that such a determination has previously been made, the judge shall immediately cause to be issued an arrest warrant or, where not prohibited by law, a summons. More than one (1) summons or warrant may issue on the same charging affidavit.

(b) Summons; Subsequent Issuance of Arrest Warrant.
(1) Summons. Unless otherwise prohibited by law, the judge may issue a summons if:

(A) the defendant is not in custody;

(B) the offense charged is bailable as a matter of right; and

(C) there is no reasonable cause to believe that the defendant will not obey the summons.

(2) Subsequent Issuance of Arrest Warrant. After the issuance of a summons, the judge shall issue an arrest warrant if:

(A) the defendant, having been duly summoned, fails to appear;

(B) there is reasonable cause to believe that the defendant will fail to appear; or

(C) the summons cannot be served or delivered for any reason.

(c) Traffic Citations Unaffected. The use of tickets, citations, or affidavits for misdemeanor traffic violations shall be as otherwise provided by law.

Comment
Rule 3.1(a) contemplates that a summons, where not prohibited by law, or arrest warrant shall issue upon a finding that a probable cause determination has been made, for example, by a competent court of another jurisdiction. *See* Miss. Code Ann. § 99-21-1.

Rule 3.1(b) gives the judge discretion to cause a summons to be issued, where not prohibited by law, in those cases in which an arrest warrant is not necessary to secure the presence of the defendant and there is little concern that the defendant will flee. Rule 3.1(b) makes no distinction between felony and misdemeanor cases.

Rule 3.1(c) provides that these Rules do not affect the use of tickets, citations, or affidavits for misdemeanor traffic violations. Traffic violations are governed by statute, e.g., the Uniform Traffic Ticket Law, Miss. Code Ann. § 63-9-21, and not these Rules.

**Rule 3.2 Contents of Arrest Warrant or Summons; Execution, Return.
(a) Arrest Warrant**. An arrest warrant issued upon a charging affidavit shall be signed by the issuing judge. The arrest warrant shall:

(1) contain the complete name of the defendant, or if the name is unknown, any name or description by which the defendant can be identified with reasonable certainty;

(2) contain the location of the defendant, if known;

(3) state the offense with which the defendant is charged; and

(4) command that the defendant be arrested and brought before the issuing judge, or, if the issuing judge is unavailable, before the nearest or most accessible judge having jurisdiction. If the defendant is bailable as a matter of right, the arrest warrant may state that the defendant shall be released on his personal recognizance, subject to the mandatory conditions of release in Rule 8.4(a), and directed to appear at a specified time and place, or be released via an appearance bond or a secured appearance bond in an amount predetermined by the court.

(b) Summons. The summons shall be in the same form as the arrest warrant, except that it shall summon the defendant to appear at a stated time and place within a reasonable time from the date of issuance.

(c) Execution of Arrest Warrant, Return.
(1) By Whom. The arrest warrant shall be directed to and may be executed by any officer authorized by law within the State of Mississippi.

(2) Manner of Execution. An arrest warrant shall be executed by arrest of the defendant.

(3) Return. After execution, the officer returning an arrest warrant shall write thereon the manner and date of execution, shall print and sign the officer's name and state the officer's badge number, and shall promptly return the arrest warrant to the clerk of the court specified in the arrest warrant.

(d) Service of Summons. The summons may be served by personally delivering a copy of the summons to the defendant by any officer authorized by law to execute arrest warrants or by delivering a copy of the summons by U.S. mail, addressed to the defendant at the defendant's usual residence, business or post office address. The officer serving the summons shall make return of the summons in the same manner as provided in Rule 3.2(c)(3) for making return of an arrest warrant.

(e) Defective Arrest Warrant. An arrest warrant shall not be invalidated nor shall any person in custody thereon be discharged because of a defect in form. The arrest warrant may be amended by the court to remedy such defect.

Comment

Where circumstances dictate issuance of an arrest warrant rather than a summons, yet there is reason for use of recognizance release, Rule 3.2(a) gives the issuing judge the flexibility of allowing a personal recognizance release, subject to the mandatory conditions of release in Rule 8.4(a). The release of an arrested defendant on recognizance would not preclude the defendant's having to appear at the initial hearing, but might preclude the defendant's spending the night in jail unnecessarily. Alternatively, the issuing judge has discretion to set an appearance bond or secured appearance bond in the warrant, if the defendant is bailable as a matter of right.

Rule 3.2(c)(1) states that an arrest warrant be directed to and executed by "any officer authorized by law within the State of Mississippi." Mississippi law authorizes a broad range of officers to make arrests. *See* Miss. Code Ann. §§ 99-3-1(1), 99-3-2.

Rule 3.2(d) is designed to make service of the summons as easy and expeditious as possible. The function of the summons is solely to apprise the defendant of the charges and to notify the defendant to appear. Delivery of a copy of the summons by U.S. mail is similar to the procedure utilized for summoning persons whose names are drawn for jury duty. *See* Miss. Code Ann. § 13-5-28. A defendant's failure to respond to a mailed summons does not provide valid grounds for the issuance of a contempt-based arrest warrant.

Under Rule 3.2(e), a mere defect in form will not invalidate an arrest warrant. Normally, aliases, fictitious names, and descriptions are matters of form and may be amended if judicially determined to be incorrect.

Rule 4 Search Warrants

Rule 4.1 Persons or Things Subject to Search and Seizure.
A search warrant may be issued for any of the following:

> (1) evidence of a crime;
>
> (2) contraband, fruits of crime, or other things unlawfully possessed;
>
> (3) thing(s) designed for use, intended for use, or which is being or has been used in committing a crime; and

(4) a person to be arrested, or who is unlawfully restrained.

Comment

Generally, Rule 4 protects the rights guaranteed by article 3, section 23, of the Mississippi Constitution ("The people shall be secure in their persons, houses, and possessions, from unreasonable seizure or search; and no warrant shall be issued without probable cause, supported by oath or affirmation, specially designating the place to be searched and the person or thing to be seized."). The Rule is broad enough to embrace the issuance of anticipatory search warrants; a warrant to search for things that are not within the jurisdiction when the warrant is issued, but that are expected to be within the jurisdiction when the search is conducted, is valid if it otherwise complies with the United States Constitution, the Mississippi Constitution, and Rule 4. *See **United States v. Grubbs***, 547 U.S. 90, 126 S. Ct. 1494, 164 L. Ed. 2d 195 (2006).

Rule 4.1 describes the persons and/or things that may be seized with a lawfully-issued search warrant. Issuance of a search warrant to search for items of solely "evidential value" is authorized. ***Warden, Md. Penitentiary v. Haden***, 387 U.S. 294, 300-01, 87 S. Ct. 1642, 1647, 18 L. Ed. 2d 782 (1967). Section (b)(4) permits issuance of a warrant to search for a person under two circumstances: when there is probable cause to arrest that person or when that person is being unlawfully restrained. There may be instances in which a search warrant would be required to conduct a search in either of these circumstances. Even when a search warrant would not be required to enter a place to search for a person, a procedure for obtaining a warrant should be available so that law enforcement officers will be encouraged to resort to the preferred alternative of acquiring "an objective predetermination of probable cause." ***Katz v. United States***, 389 U.S. 347, 88 S. Ct. 507, 19 L. Ed. 2d 576 (1967).

Rule 4.2 Warrant on Affidavit.
(a) In General. No search warrant shall issue except upon affidavit presented to the issuing judge authorized by law to issue search warrants, establishing grounds for issuing the warrant.

(b) Issuance. If the judge finds probable cause exists, the judge shall issue a warrant naming or describing the person or thing to be seized, and naming or describing the person or place to be searched.

Comment

Under section (b), probable cause for the issuance of a search warrant should be assessed under the totality-of-circumstances test. *See Jordan v. State*, 995 So. 2d 94 (Miss. 2008); *Illinois v. Gates*, 462 U.S. 213, 103 S. Ct. 2317, 76 L. Ed. 2d 527 (1983).

Rule 4.3 Contents of Search Warrants.

Every search warrant issued by the court shall:

(1) command the law enforcement officer to search, within a specified time not to exceed ten (10) days, the person(s) or place(s) named in the search warrant and to return the warrant and an inventory of the thing(s) seized to the court as designated in the warrant;

(2) designate the court to which the warrant and an inventory of the thing(s) seized shall be returned; and

(3) be signed and dated by the judge, showing the exact time and date and the name of the law enforcement officer to whom the warrant was delivered for execution.

Comment

The ten (10) day requirement in section (a) is consistent with the long-standing holding that "some date, within a reasonable time after the issuance of the warrant, be fixed for its return, and that it should be executed within the time within which it is, by its terms, a live process." *Taylor v. State*, 137 Miss. 217, 102 So. 267, 268 (1924). The Court has also recognized that search warrants shall be returnable instanter or on a day stated. *See Meyer v. State*, 309 So. 2d 161, 165-66 (Miss. 1975) (return two (2) days after the search warrant was served was not a breach of the statutory requirement that warrant be executed and returned within ten (10) days and was not an unreasonable delay); *Jordan v. State*, 147 Miss. 24, 112 So. 590 (1927) (the requirement that the warrant should be returned instanter only required that it should be executed and returned within a reasonable time under the circumstances of the case, and that the execution of a search warrant on the day following the date of its issuance sufficiently complies with the mandate that it be executed and returned instanter). The requirement that a search warrant be executed within a reasonable time prevents the search warrant from being "held by an officer as a weapon, to be used at his discretion." *Taylor*, 102 So. at 268. Pursuant to Rule 4.3, even an anticipatory search warrant must be executed within ten (10) days of the date the search warrant was issued.

Rule 4.4 Execution and Return with Inventory; Return of Papers to Court; Custody of Things.
(a) Receipt and Inventory. The law enforcement officer conducting the search under the search warrant shall give to the person from whom or from whose premises the things were taken, or shall leave at the place from which the things were taken, a copy of the search warrant together with a copy of an inventory of the things taken. The inventory shall be made in the presence of the person from whose possession or premises the things were taken, if that person is present, and shall be verified by the law enforcement officer executing the search warrant.

(b) Return of Papers to Court. The law enforcement officer executing the search warrant shall promptly return the search warrant, along with any inventory of things seized, to the court specified in the search warrant. Unexecuted search warrants shall be returned to the court.

(c) Custody of Things. All things taken pursuant to a search warrant shall be retained in the custody of the seizing officer or agency, subject to court order.

Comment
Section (a) is intended to make clear that a copy of the warrant and an inventory receipt for things taken shall be left at the premises at the time of the search or with the person, if present, from whose premises the things are taken.

Section (b) requires prompt return of the executed warrant and inventory. *See Brown v. State*, 534 So. 2d 1019 (Miss. 1988) (describing return as ministerial act and noting improper return does not invalidate search).

Rule 5 Arrest and Initial Appearance

Rule 5.1 Procedure upon Arrest.

(a) Telephone Call. Any person under arrest shall be afforded a reasonable opportunity to make a telephone call to, or otherwise make effective communication with, any person the accused may choose.

(b) On Arrest without a Warrant. A person arrested without a warrant:

> (1) may, unless prohibited by law, be released upon the defendant's personal recognizance after being notified in writing to appear at a specified time and place; or

> (2) shall be released upon execution of an appearance bond set according to Rule 8, unless the charge upon which the person was arrested is not a bailable offense, and directed to appear at a specified time and place; or

> (3) if not released pursuant to subsections (b)(1) or (b)(2), the accused shall be taken without unnecessary delay, and in no event later than forty-eight (48) hours after arrest, before a judge for an initial appearance. If the person arrested is not taken before a judge as so required then, unless the offense for which the person was arrested is not a bailable offense, the person shall be released upon execution of an appearance bond in the amount of the minimum bail specified in Rule 8, and shall be directed to appear at a specified time and place.

In the event the defendant is released on the minimum amount provided in the bail schedule, the prosecuting attorney may file a motion with the court to reconsider the bond amount and the conditions of release, and the procedures thereafter shall be in accordance with Rule 8.

(c) On Arrest with a Warrant.

(1) If provision for bail or personal recognizance has been made by the judge issuing the arrest warrant, a person arrested with a warrant shall be released and directed to appear at a specified time and place.

(2) If the person arrested cannot meet the conditions of release provided in the warrant, or if no such conditions are prescribed:

> (A) if such person was arrested pursuant to a warrant issued on a charging affidavit, the accused shall be taken without unnecessary delay, and in no event later than forty-eight (48) hours after arrest, before a judge for an initial appearance. If the person arrested has not been taken before a judge as required herein, unless the charge upon which the person was arrested is not a bailable offense, such person shall be released upon execution of an appearance bond in the amount of the minimum bail specified in Rule 8, and shall be notified in writing to appear at a specified time and place; or

> (B) if such person was arrested pursuant to a capias issued upon an indictment, the accused shall be taken without unnecessary delay before a judge, who shall proceed as provided in Rule 8.

(3) The defendant shall be given a copy of the charging document.

Comment

Rule 5.1(a) gives official sanction to common existing practice. The opportunity to make a telephone call represents the minimum requirement and use of other appropriate means of communication, electronic or otherwise, may be allowed. Fundamental fairness dictates that a person who has been taken into custody be allowed to communicate to another that the accused is being held by the police and charged with a crime. Rule 5.1(a) thus serves to protect an accused's state and federal constitutional rights to bail, counsel, and due process.

Rule 5.1(b) lists the options available to law enforcement officers in the case of warrantless arrests. An officer may: (1) release the offender on personal recognizance and issue a notice requiring the person to appear at a specified time and place; (2) release the offender on execution of an appearance bond set according to Rule 8 and direct the person to appear at a specified time and place; or (3) take the offender into custody and provide the person with an opportunity to make bail. A person may not be released on personal recognizance where prohibited by law. *See, e.g.,* Miss. Code Ann. § 99-5-37 (regarding arrest for listed domestic violence offenses).

Under Rule 5.1(b)(3), if a person is taken into custody, the person shall be taken without unnecessary delay, and in no event later than forty-eight (48) hours after arrest, before a judge who shall proceed with an initial appearance. If the person arrested is not taken before a judge within forty-eight (48) hours, the person detained shall be released on execution of an appearance bond in the minimum amount set pursuant to Rule 8 and directed to appear at a specified time and place. Rule 5.1(b)(3) conforms to the United States Supreme Court's holdings in *Gerstein v. Pugh*, 420 U.S. 103, 95 S. Ct. 854, 43 L. Ed. 2d 54 (1975), and *County of Riverside v. McLaughlin*, 500 U.S. 44, 111 S. Ct. 1661, 114 L. Ed. 2d 49 (1991).

Rule 5.2 Initial Appearance.

(a) Generally. Every person in custody and not under indictment shall be taken, without unnecessary delay and in accordance with Rule 5.1, before a judge for an initial appearance. At the defendant's initial appearance, the judge shall:

> (1) ascertain the defendant's true name, age, and address, and amend the formal charge if necessary to reflect this information, instructing the defendant to notify the court promptly of any change of address;

(2) inform the defendant of the charges and provide the defendant with a copy of the charging affidavit;

(3) if the arrest has been made without a warrant, determine whether there was probable cause for the arrest and note the probable cause determination for the record. If there was no probable cause for the warrantless arrest, the defendant shall be released;

(4) if the defendant is unrepresented, advise of the right to assistance of an attorney, and that if the defendant is unable to afford an attorney, an attorney will be appointed as required by law. If the indigent defendant is unrepresented and desires representation, counsel shall be appointed pursuant to Rule 7.2, Rule 7.3 and local rule promulgated pursuant to Rule 1.9; and

(5) advise the defendant of:

> (A) the right to remain silent and that any statements made may be used against the defendant;
>
> (B) the right to communicate with an attorney, family or friends, and that reasonable means will be provided to enable the defendant to do so; and
>
> (C) the conditions, if any, under which the defendant may obtain release.

(b) Felony Cases. When a defendant is charged with commission of a felony, the judge shall also:

> (1) inform the defendant of the right to a preliminary hearing and the procedure by which that right may be exercised; and
>
> (2) if requested, set the time for a preliminary hearing in accordance with Rule 6.1.

(c) Initial Appearance Not Required. In all cases where the defendant is released from custody, or has been indicted by a grand jury, the defendant shall not be entitled to an initial appearance.

Comment

The purpose of Rule 5.2 is to insert the judicial process between the police and the defendant at the earliest practicable time in order to minimize the effects of carelessness, abuse of power, or unavoidable error in the police function. Rule 5.2 insures procedural compliance with *Miranda v. Arizona*, 384 U.S. 436, 86 S. Ct. 1602, 16 L. Ed. 2d 694 (1966), and *Escobedo v. Illinois*, 378 U.S. 478, 84 S. Ct. 1758, 12 L. Ed. 2d 977 (1964), and provides for the prompt determination of the conditions for release. This continues the policy contained in Mississippi Code Section 99-3-17 and former Rule 6.03 of the Uniform Rules of Circuit and County Court.

Pursuant to Rule 1.8, with the defendant's consent, initial appearances may be held via interactive audiovisual devices.

Rule 5.2(c) underscores that a defendant who has been released from custody, or who has been indicted, is not entitled to an initial appearance. This continues the practice provided in former Rule 6.05 of the Uniform Rules of Circuit and County Court.

Rule 6 Preliminary Hearing

Rule 6.1 Right to a Preliminary Hearing; Waiver; Postponement.
(a) Right to a Preliminary Hearing.
(1) Generally. A defendant who has been charged with a felony is entitled to a preliminary hearing upon request. But a defendant who has been indicted by a grand jury is not entitled to a preliminary hearing.

(2) When Commenced. The preliminary hearing shall be held within fourteen (14) days following the demand for preliminary hearing unless:

(A) the charging affidavit has been dismissed;

(B) the hearing is subsequently waived, as provided in section (b);

(C) the hearing is postponed as provided in section (d); or

(D) before commencement of the hearing, an indictment charging the same offense has been returned by the grand jury.

(b) Waiver. A preliminary hearing, once demanded, may be subsequently waived in open court or by written waiver, signed by the defendant and defendant's counsel, if any.

(c) Delay.
(1) Release on Recognizance. If a preliminary hearing has not been commenced within fourteen (14) days as required by subsection (a), unless postponed as provided in subsection (d), the defendant shall be released on recognizance.

(2) Non-bailable Offenses; Notice to Circuit Court. However, if the defendant is charged with a non-bailable offense, or if release is prohibited by Article 3, Section 29(2) of the Mississippi Constitution of 1890, the court, the attorneys, or the accused, if *pro se*, shall immediately notify a judge of that circuit of the delay and the reasons therefor. The circuit judge shall thereupon order the hearing be set for a specified time.

(d) Postponement. Upon motion of any party, or upon the judge's own initiative, the preliminary hearing may be postponed beyond the time limits specified in subsection (a) upon a finding that circumstances exist that justify delay and, in that event, the court shall enter a written order detailing the reasons for the finding, include a date certain for the postponed hearing, and shall give the parties prompt notice thereof.

Comment

Rule 6.1(a) grants an accused charged with a felony (and not under indictment) the right to a preliminary hearing upon request. *See* ***Mayfield v.***

State, 612 So. 2d 1120, 1129 (Miss. 1992) (the principal purpose of a preliminary hearing is to determine whether probable cause exists). The provision that a defendant who has been indicted by a grand jury is not entitled to a preliminary hearing is consistent with former Rule 6.05 of the Uniform Rules of Circuit and County Court.

Rule 6.1(c) states that if a preliminary hearing is not commenced within fourteen (14) days as required by subsection (a), and is not postponed as allowed by subsection (d), the defendant shall be released on recognizance, unless the offense is non-bailable or release is prohibited by Article 3, Section 29(2) of the Mississippi Constitution of 1890.

Rule 6.2 Proceedings at Preliminary Hearing.
(a) Procedure. At a preliminary hearing the judge shall determine probable cause and the conditions for release, if any. All parties shall have the right to cross-examine the witnesses testifying and, subject to the provisions herein, introduce evidence. Only evidence relevant to these questions shall be adduced.

At the close of the prosecution's case, including cross-examination of prosecution witnesses by the defendant, the judge shall determine and state for the record or state in open court whether the prosecution's case establishes probable cause. The defendant may then make a specific offer of proof, including the names of witnesses who would testify, or the defendant may produce the evidence offered.

(b) Process. Unless otherwise ordered by the court for good cause shown, process shall issue to secure the attendance of witnesses requested by the defendant or the prosecuting attorney.

(c) Hearsay Evidence. The findings by the court shall be based on substantial evidence, which may be hearsay, in whole or in part, provided there is a basis for believing the source of the hearsay to be credible and for believing that there is a factual basis for the information furnished.

(d) Suppression Motions Inapplicable. Objections to evidence on the ground that it was acquired by unlawful means are not properly made at the preliminary hearing.

(e) Amendment of Charging Affidavit. The charging affidavit may be amended at any time to conform to the evidence, unless substantial rights of the defendant would be prejudiced.

(f) Binding Over the Case to the Grand Jury. If, from the evidence, it appears that there is probable cause to believe that a felony has been committed, and that the defendant committed it, the judge shall bind the defendant over to await action of the grand jury.

(g) Discharge of the Defendant. If, from the evidence, it appears that there is no probable cause to believe that a felony has been committed or that the defendant committed it, the defendant shall be discharged from custody. The discharge of the defendant shall not preclude the state from presenting the same offense to a grand jury.

Comment

Rule 6.2(a) limits the issues at a preliminary hearing to probable cause and the conditions of release. A defendant is permitted to cross-examine witnesses and present testimony and evidence. Rule 6.2(b) complements these rights by providing defendants with process to secure the attendance of witnesses, unless otherwise ordered by the court on a showing of good cause.

Rule 6.2(c) notes the admissibility of hearsay, which is in accord with Rule 1101(b)(4) of the Mississippi Rules of Evidence (except for rules pertaining to privileges, the rules of evidence are inapplicable in probable cause hearings in criminal cases). There is no constitutional requirement that hearsay evidence be excluded from a probable cause hearing. *See* ***Conerly v. State***, 760 So. 2d 737, 740-41 (Miss. 2000) (determination of probable cause may be based on corroborated and substantiated hearsay); ***Costello v. United States***, 350 U.S. 359, 76 S. Ct. 406, 100 L. Ed. 397 (1956) (upholding a grand jury indictment based solely on hearsay testimony).

Rule 7 Counsel

Rule 7.1 Right to Counsel; Waiver.

(a) Right to be Represented by Counsel. A defendant shall be entitled to be represented by counsel in any criminal proceeding. The right to be represented shall include the right to consult in private with an attorney or the attorney's agent, without unnecessary delay, after a defendant is taken into custody, at reasonable times thereafter, and sufficiently in advance of a proceeding to allow adequate preparation therefor.

(b) Right to Appointed Counsel. An indigent defendant shall be entitled to have an attorney appointed in any criminal proceeding which may result in punishment by loss of liberty, in any other criminal proceeding in which the court concludes that the interests of justice so require, or as required by law. The determination of the right to appointed counsel, and the appointment of such counsel, is to be made no later than at the indigent defendant's first appearance before a judge.

(c) Waiver of Right to Counsel. When the court learns that a defendant desires to act as his/her own attorney, the court shall conduct an on-the-record examination of the defendant to determine if the defendant knowingly and voluntarily desires to act as his/her own attorney. The court shall inform the defendant that:

> 1. The defendant has a right to an attorney, and if the defendant cannot afford an attorney, then the court will appoint one free of charge to defend or assist the defendant in his/her defense.

> 2. The defendant has the right to conduct the defense and may elect to do so and allow whatever role (s)he desires to his/her attorney.

> 3. The court will not relax or disregard the rules of evidence, procedure or courtroom protocol for the defendant and that the defendant will be bound by and have to conduct himself/herself

within the same rules as an attorney, that these rules are not simple and that without legal advice his/her ability to defend himself/herself will be hampered.

4. The right to proceed *pro se* usually increases the likelihood of a trial outcome unfavorable to the defendant.

5. Other matters as the court deems appropriate.

After informing the defendant and ascertaining that the defendant understands these matters, the court will ascertain whether the defendant still wishes to proceed *pro se* or if the defendant desires an attorney to assist him/her in his/her defense. If the defendant desires to proceed *pro se*, the court should determine whether the defendant has exercised this right knowingly and voluntarily and, if so, make the finding a matter of record. At the time of accepting a defendant's waiver of the right to counsel, the court shall inform the defendant that the waiver may be withdrawn and counsel appointed or retained at any stage of the proceedings. Additionally, the court may appoint an attorney to assist the defendant on procedure and protocol, even if the defendant does not desire an attorney. Such advisory counsel shall be given notice of all matters of which the defendant is notified.

(d) Withdrawal of Waiver. A defendant may withdraw a waiver of the right to counsel at any stage of the proceedings but will not be entitled to repeat any proceeding previously held or waived solely on the grounds of the subsequent appointment or retention of counsel.

(e) Unreasonable Delay in Retaining Counsel. If a non-indigent defendant appears without counsel at any proceeding after having been given reasonable time to retain counsel, the cause may proceed. If an indigent defendant who has refused appointed counsel in order to obtain private counsel appears without counsel at any proceeding after having been given reasonable time to retain counsel, the court shall appoint counsel unless the indigent defendant waives the right under section (c). If the indigent defendant continues to refuse appointed counsel, the cause may proceed.

Comment

Rule 7.1 establishes guidelines for the representation of both indigent and non-indigent criminal defendants. The basis of Rule 7.1 is the right of an accused to be represented by counsel in all criminal prosecutions. *See* U.S. Const. amend. VI ("In all criminal prosecutions, the accused shall enjoy the right . . . to have the assistance of counsel for his defence."); Miss. Const. art. 3, § 26 ("In all criminal prosecutions the accused shall have a right to be heard by himself or counsel, or both . . . .").

For the purposes of subsection (a), the term "criminal proceeding" includes any stage of the criminal process, without regard to whether a "criminal proceeding" has or has not been commenced under Rule 2.1. The provision that a defendant may consult with the attorney's agent is added for the attorney's convenience.

Rule 7.1(b) is adopted from *Gideon v. Wainwright*, 372 U.S. 335, 83 S. Ct. 792, 9 L. Ed. 2d 799 (1963); *Argersinger v. Hamlin*, 407 U.S. 25, 92 S. Ct. 2006, 32 L. Ed. 2d 530 (1972); and Mississippi Code Section 99-15-15. *See also Alabama v. Shelton*, 535 U.S. 654, 661-62, 122 S. Ct. 1764, 1769-70, 152 L. Ed. 2d 888 (2002).

Under section (b), there are two pertinent inquiries in determining when counsel is to be appointed to represent an indigent defendant. The first inquiry is whether the right to appointed counsel arises at all. *See Dunn v. State*, 693 So. 2d 1333, 1339 (Miss. 1997) (citing *Scott v. Illinois*, 440 U.S. 367, 374, 99 S. Ct. 1158, 1162, 59 L. Ed. 2d 383 (1979)). The second inquiry is if the defendant is entitled to appointed counsel, at what point in the process is counsel to be appointed. Regarding this second inquiry, Mississippi law provides that "[t]he accused shall have such representation at every critical stage of the proceedings . . . where a substantial right may be affected." Miss. Code Ann. § 25-32-9(2). Specifically:

> [u]nder Mississippi law, the right to counsel attaches earlier than does the sixth amendment right. *Williamson* [*v. State*], 512 So. 2d [868,] 876 [(Miss. 1987)]; *Page v. State*, 495 So. 2d 436, 439

(Miss. 1986). This right attaches "once the proceedings against the defendant reach the accusatory stage." **Williamson**, 512 So. 2d at 876; **Page**, 495 So. 2d at 439. The "accusatory stage" is defined by Mississippi law to occur when a warrant is issued or, "by binding over or recognizing the offender to compel his appearance to answer the offense, as well as by indictment or affidavit." Miss. Code Ann. § 99-1-7 (1972). This right to counsel [also] "attaches at the point in time when 'the initial appearance . . . *ought to have been held. . . .*'" **Veal** [*v. State*], 585 So.2d [693,] 699 [(Miss. 1991)] (emphasis added).

Ormond v. State, 599 So. 2d 951, 956 (Miss. 1992). *See also* **Weeks v. State**, 804 So. 2d 980, 995 (Miss. 2001); **Sanders v. State**, 801 So. 2d 694, 700 (Miss. 2001) (citing **Johnson v. State**, 631 So. 2d 185, 187-88 (Miss. 1994)) ("The Sixth Amendment right to counsel attaches once the proceedings reach the accusatory stage.").

Rule 7.1(c) provides the standards for waiver of the right to counsel, applicable throughout these rules. It is derived from former Rule 8.05 of the Uniform Rules of Circuit and County Court and adopts the constitutional standard set down in **Johnson v. Zerbst**, 304 U.S. 458, 58 S. Ct. 1019, 82 L. Ed. 1461 (1938); **Von Moltke v. Gillies**, 332 U.S. 708, 68 S. Ct. 316, 92 L. Ed. 309 (1948); and **Argersinger**, and followed by the Mississippi Supreme Court in **Conn v. State**, 251 Miss. 488, 170 So. 2d 20 (1964). *See also* **Bradley v. State**, 58 So. 3d 1166, 1170 (Miss. 2011); **Patton v. State**, 34 So. 3d 563, 565-69 (Miss. 2010).

Subsection (c) also allows, but does not require, the court to appoint advisory or standby counsel. Although a criminal defendant has an absolute right to defend *pro se* under the Sixth Amendment, there may be instances where a court will deem the appointment of standby counsel advisable and in the defendant's best interest. *See* **Patton**, 34 So. 3d at 567; **McKaskle v. Wiggins**, 465 U.S. 168, 104 S. Ct. 944, 79 L. Ed. 2d 122 (1984); **Faretta v. California**, 422 U.S. 806, 95 S. Ct. 2525, 45 L. Ed. 2d 562 (1975); **United States v. Theriault**, 474 F. 2d 359 (5th Cir. 1973), *cert. denied*, 411 U.S. 984 (1973).

Under Rule 7.1(d), the defendant can decide at any stage of the proceedings that it was a mistake to waive counsel. The court should encourage an unrepresented defendant, at all stages, to obtain counsel. But while the defendant's right to withdraw waiver of counsel is unlimited, a defendant is not allowed to use late appointment or retention of counsel to disrupt orderly and timely processing of the case. Thus, a defendant cannot delay a scheduled proceeding, nor repeat one already held, solely because of a change of heart concerning the need for counsel.

Rule 7.1(e) protects the court against dilatory tactics by the defendant in retaining counsel while at the same time preserving the defendant's right to counsel. *See Sample v. State*, 320 So. 2d 801, 804 (Miss. 1975) ("We recognize that the defendant must be given a reasonable opportunity to employ and consult with the attorney of his choosing."). It allows an indigent defendant the opportunity to make a good faith, though unsuccessful, effort to obtain private counsel, even though the proceeding may be delayed. *See McConnell v. United States*, 375 F. 2d 905 (5th Cir. 1967); *Cleveland v. United States*, 322 F. 2d 401 (D.C. Cir. 1963), *cert. denied*, 375 U.S. 884 (1963).

Rule 7.2 Procedure for Appointment of Counsel for Indigent Defendants; Appearance; Withdrawal.
(a) Procedure for Appointment of Counsel for Indigent Defendants.
(1) Generally. A procedure shall be established in each circuit, county, municipal, and justice court for the appointment of counsel for each indigent defendant entitled thereto.

(2) Appointment of Multiple Attorneys. In all death penalty trial proceedings, the court shall appoint two (2) attorneys pursuant to the standards in Rule 7.4. At the time of the appointment, and subject to court approval, the appointed attorney may recommend co-counsel so long as co-counsel is willing to accept the appointment and meets all of the requirements of Rule 7.4. If the appointed attorney does not recommend co-counsel upon accepting an appointment, the court shall select co-counsel. In non-death penalty cases, the appointment of multiple attorneys is within the discretion of the court.

(b) Entry of Appearance. At or before a first appearance in any court on behalf of a defendant, an attorney, whether privately retained or court-appointed, shall file an entry of appearance or, in lieu thereof, the court shall note the attorney's appearance on the record.

(c) Duty of Continuing Representation. Counsel representing a defendant at any stage following indictment shall continue to represent that defendant in all further proceedings in the trial court, including filing a notice of appeal, unless counsel withdraws for good cause as approved by the court.

(d) Withdrawal. When an attorney makes an appearance for any party in a case, that attorney will not be allowed to withdraw as attorney for the party without the permission of the court. The attorney making the request shall give notice to his/her client and to all attorneys in the cause and certify the same to the court in writing. The court shall not permit withdrawal without prior notice to his/her client and all attorneys of record.

Comment

Rule 7.2(a) requires that each circuit shall establish governing local procedures for the appointment of counsel for indigent defendants. Local court rules are promulgated pursuant to Rule 1.9.

Rule 7.2(c) contemplates that the usual procedure will be that, following indictment, counsel will continue to represent the defendant through all stages of the trial proceedings, including filing a notice of appeal. *See* M.R.A.P. 6(b). In addition to being familiar with the case, continued representation guarantees that a defendant's right of appeal is not lost in the period between termination of trial counsel's responsibilities and retention or appointment of appellate counsel.

Rule 7.2(d) is consistent with former Rule 1.13 of the Uniform Rules of Circuit and County Court Practice. Normally, appointed counsel will not be permitted to withdraw prior to filing a notice of appeal. If the court allows counsel to withdraw, the court shall see that new counsel is retained or appointed, unless the right to counsel has been properly waived pursuant to Rule

7.1(c). In this way, subsection (d) maintains the integrity of the trial date, while also protecting the interests of the defendant and aiding the trial court in providing continuity in legal representation.

Nothing in Rules 7.2(c) or (d) limits the ability of a court to appoint an attorney to represent a defendant for a limited purpose or time, after which another attorney is appointed or retained to represent the defendant for subsequent proceedings.

Rule 7.3   Determination of Indigency; Appointment of Counsel; Compensation.
(a) Standard for Indigency. The term "indigent" as used in these Rules means a person who is financially unable to employ counsel.

(b) Affidavit or Sworn Testimony of Substantial Hardship. A defendant desiring to proceed as an indigent may complete an affidavit concerning the defendant's financial resources on a court-approved form.   In lieu of an affidavit, or together with an affidavit, the defendant may be examined under oath regarding defendant's financial resources by the judge responsible for determining indigency. Before said questioning, the defendant shall be advised of the penalties for perjury as provided by law.

(c) Reconsideration. Following a determination of indigency or non-indigency, if there has been a material change in circumstances, the defendant, the appointed attorney, or the prosecutor may move for reconsideration.

(d) Order of Appointment. Whenever counsel is appointed, the court shall enter an order to that effect, a copy of which shall be provided to the defendant, the appointed attorney, and the prosecutor.

(e) Appointment of Public Defender. In counties or municipalities which have a public defender, the public defender shall represent all defendants entitled to appointed counsel whenever authorized by law and able to do so.

(f) Other Appointments. If the public defender is not appointed, a private attorney shall be appointed to the case. All criminal appointments shall be made in a manner fair and equitable to the members of the bar, taking into account the skill likely to be required in handling a particular case.

(g) Appointment of Counsel During Appeal Following Withdrawal. When prior counsel is permitted to withdraw, the trial or appellate court shall appoint new counsel for a defendant legally entitled to such representation on appeal.

(h) Compensation. A private attorney appointed to represent an indigent defendant is entitled to compensation for services rendered as provided by law. Other than compensation for services rendered as provided by law, no appointed counsel may request or accept any payment or promise of payment for assisting in the representation of a defendant.

(i) Expenses. Appointed counsel shall be entitled to reasonable and necessary expenses incurred in defense of an indigent client, including fees and expenses of expert or professional persons, provided that such expenses are approved in the sound discretion of the court. Extraordinary expenses, including expert expenses, shall be approved in advance by the court.

Comment

Rule 7.3 establishes a procedure for the determination of indigency. In making a determination of indigency, the court should consider factors such as the defendant's income and sources of income; employment status; real or personal property owned; outstanding obligations; and the number and age(s) of any dependant(s). *See* Miss. Code Ann. § 25-32-9(1). The court shall not consider the fact that the defendant has been released on bond, or the financial ability of friends or relatives not legally responsible for the defendant.

Rule 7.3(e) establishes the rule for appointment of public defenders rather than private counsel in counties or municipalities that have a public defender's office. *See* Miss. Code Ann. § 25-32-9(1). When the public defender's office cannot represent an indigent defendant (e.g., when there is a conflict of interest or the public defender is unable to provide prompt and adequate representation), private counsel shall be appointed. *See* Miss. Code Ann. § 25-32-13.

Rule 7.3(g) provides for continuity of representation by requiring the trial or appellate court to appoint new counsel for a defendant legally entitled to such representation on appeal, when prior counsel is permitted to withdraw. *See* M.R.A.P. 6(b); ***Jones v. State***, 355 So. 2d 89, 91 (Miss. 1978) ("An accused is not only entitled to counsel at trial, but he is entitled to counsel on appeal from a conviction on the merits. If he is indigent and unable to afford an attorney, then he is entitled to a court-appointed attorney at trial and on appeal.").

Rule 7.3(h) is consistent with existing law regarding the compensation of appointed counsel. *See* Miss. Code Ann. § 99-15-17. Rule 7.3(i) addresses the reimbursement of reasonable and necessary expenses to appointed counsel. *See* Miss. Code Ann. §§ 99-15-17, 99-15-21; ***Howell v. State***, 989 So. 2d 372, 390 (Miss. 2008) (quoting ***Ruffin v. State***, 447 So. 2d 113, 118 (Miss. 1984)) ("[a]n indigent's . . . right to defense expenses . . . is conditioned upon a showing that such expenses are needed to prepare and present an adequate defense"); ***Hansen v. State***, 592 So. 2d 114, 125 (Miss. 1991) (State must pay for "non-legal personnel needed by the defense" on showing of "substantial need"); ***Wilson v. State***, 574 So. 2d 1338, 1341 (Miss. 1990).

Rule 7.4 Standards for Appointment of Trial and Appellate Counsel in Death Penalty Cases.

(a) In General. To be eligible for appointment in a death penalty case, an attorney:

> (1) shall have been a member in good standing of the State Bar of Mississippi for at least five (5) years immediately preceding the appointment, or admitted *pro hac vice* pursuant to an order entered under Rule 46 of the Mississippi Rules of Appellate Procedure and be a member in good standing of that attorney's home jurisdiction for a like period immediately preceding the appointment;

(2) shall have practiced in the area of state criminal litigation for three (3) years immediately preceding the appointment;

(3) shall have in the three (3) years before appointment completed twelve (12) hours of training or educational programs in the area of death penalty defense through a program accredited by the Mississippi Commission on Continuing Legal Education or the American Bar Association; and

(4) shall have demonstrated the necessary proficiency and commitment to zealous advocacy which exemplify the quality of representation appropriate to death penalty cases.

(b) Additional Qualification Requirements.
At least one (1) appointed attorney must meet the qualifications set forth in section (a) and the following:

(1) shall have practiced in the area of state criminal litigation for five (5) years immediately preceding the appointment; and

(2) shall have been counsel in at least five (5) felony jury trials that were tried to completion, including at least one (1) death penalty murder jury trial that was tried to completion in which the attorney participated.

(c) Appellate Counsel. To be eligible for appointment as appellate counsel on behalf of a defendant sentenced to death, an attorney must meet the qualifications set forth in section (a) and, within five (5) years immediately preceding the appointment, have been counsel in an appeal or post-conviction proceeding in a case in which a death sentence was imposed, as well as have experience as counsel in the appeal of at least three (3) felony convictions. Alternatively, an attorney must have been counsel in the appeal of at least six (6) felony convictions, at least two (2) of which were appeals from murder convictions.

(d) Exceptional Circumstances. In exceptional circumstances enumerated by the trial judge on the record, an attorney may be appointed who does not meet the qualifications set forth in sections (a)(1)-(3), (b) and/or (c), provided that the attorney's experience, stature and record in a different type of practice (e.g., civil litigation, academic work, or work for a court or prosecutor) enable the court to conclude that the attorney's ability meets or exceeds the standards set forth in this Rule.

Comment

The purpose of Rule 7.4 is to establish standards for appointment of counsel for indigent defendants in the trial and appellate stages of capital litigation. The provisions of this rule generally parallel the qualifications set forth in Rule 22 of the Mississippi Rules of Appellate Procedure regarding qualifications for capital post-conviction counsel.

Rule 7.4(b) establishes elevated standards for at least one (1) of the appointed attorneys. Rule 7.4(c) sets out standards for counsel in appellate proceedings. (Of course, Rule 22 of the Mississippi Rules of Appellate Procedure, not Rule 7.4(c), governs appointment of capital post-conviction counsel.) Rule 7.2(a)(2) requires that co-counsel be appointed in all death penalty trial proceedings; co-counsel should ordinarily be appointed at the appellate stage as well.

Rule 8 Release

Rule 8.1 Definitions and Requirements.
Whenever the terms below appear in these Rules, they shall have the following meanings:
(a) Personal Recognizance. A release on defendant's "personal recognizance" means release without any condition relating to, or a deposit of, security.

(b) Unsecured Appearance Bond. An "unsecured appearance bond" is an undertaking to pay a specified sum of money to the clerk of the circuit, county, justice, or municipal court, for the use of the State of Mississippi or the municipality, on the failure of a person released to comply with its conditions.

(c) Secured Appearance Bond. A "secured appearance bond" is an appearance bond secured by deposit with the clerk of security equal to the full amount thereof.

(d) Cash Deposit Bond. A "cash deposit bond" is an appearance bond secured by deposit with the clerk of security, in the form of a cash deposit or certified funds, in an amount set by the judge. The following requirements shall be met for a cash deposit bond:

(1) The accused must never have been convicted in any court of this state, another state or a federal court, of a crime punishable by more than one (1) year's imprisonment, currently is not charged with or previously been convicted of escape, or had an order *nisi* entered on a previous bond;

(2) The amount of the bond must be set by the proper authority;

(3) A return date must be set by the proper authority;

(4) The accused must tender to the clerk of the circuit court ten percent (10%) of the amount of the bond as set, in cash, or $250.00 in cash, whichever is greater;

(5) The accused must sign an appearance bond guaranteeing his/her appearance and binding himself/herself unto the State of Mississippi in the full amount of the bond as set to be used in the case of default;

(6) The accused, by affidavit duly notarized, must swear in substantially the following form:

State of Mississippi

County of _____

Personally appeared before me, the undersigned authority in and for said county and state, _____, who after being duly sworn states:

(a) I have never been convicted in any court of this state, another state, or a federal court of a crime punishable by more than one (1) year's imprisonment. I am not charged with escape and I have never been convicted of escape. I have had no order *nisi* entered on a bail bond executed by me.

(b) The proper authority has set the sum of $_____ as the amount of bail bond to be executed by me. This bond was set by _____.

(c) A return date has been set for this bond. Its return date is _____ and was set by _____.

(d) I have tendered to the clerk of the Circuit Court of _____ County, Mississippi, ten percent (10%) of the amount of said bond in cash, which sum is not less than $250.00. Said cash is my property. I authorize the clerk of said court to dispose of the same as follows: If the bond is forfeited, the cash tendered will be paid by the clerk, less a fee of not more than $10.00, to the county, and the amount so paid will be credited on the bond forfeited. If I appear on the return day and a final disposition is made of the case, the amount deposited with the clerk, less a fee of not more than $10.00 to be retained by the clerk, will be disposed of as ordered by the court.

(e) I agree to report to the clerk of the court by telephone, or in person, and in writing on the first Monday of each month as to my current address and telephone number. If I fail to do so, I agree that the bond may be declared in default.

(7) The amount of money tendered under this rule shall not be disbursed to any person except on written order of the court. The money deposited with the clerk shall be disbursed in the following manner: first, to pay any court costs assessed against the defendant; second, to pay any restitution the defendant has been ordered to make; third, to pay any fines imposed against the defendant; fourth, to pay any assignment of the sum made by the defendant to defendant's attorney; and fifth, any refund to the defendant or other disbursements as allowed by the court.

(e) Security. "Security" is cash, certified funds, or a surety's undertaking deposited with the clerk to secure an appearance bond.

(f) Surety. A "surety" is someone (other than the person seeking release) who executes an appearance bond and is therefore bound to pay its amount, if the person released fails to appear for any proceeding as ordered by the court. A surety, except one governed by Mississippi Code Section 83-39-1 *et. seq.*, shall file with the appearance bond an affidavit or sworn certification:

(1) stating that the surety is not an attorney, judicial official, or person authorized to accept bail;

(2) stating that the surety owns property in this state, which property, standing alone or when aggregated with that of other sureties, is worth the amount of the appearance bond (provided, that the property shall be exclusive of property exempt from execution and its value equaling the amount of the appearance bond shall be above and over all liabilities, including the amount of all other outstanding appearance bonds entered into by the surety) and

specifying that property and the exemptions and liabilities thereon; and

(3) specifying the number and amount of other outstanding appearance bonds entered into by the surety.

Generally, an attorney, judicial official, or person authorized to accept bail (e.g., a sheriff) may not be a surety. However, an attorney, judicial official, or person authorized to accept bail may be a surety for a member of the surety's immediate family. For purposes of this Rule, the term "immediate family" shall be limited to include only: a spouse, a sibling, a spouse's sibling, a lineal ancestor or descendant, a lineal ancestor or descendant of a spouse, or a minor or incompetent person dependent upon the surety for more than one-half ($\frac{1}{2}$) of his/her support. In such cases, the attorney, judicial official, or person authorized to accept bail shall file with the appearance bond an affidavit stating the surety's position, the surety's relationship to the person seeking release, and the information required in Rule 8.1(f)(2) and (3).

(g) Bail. "Bail" is a monetary amount for or condition of pretrial release from custody, normally set by a judge at the initial appearance.

(h) Insurer. The terms "insurer," "professional bail agent," "soliciting bail agent," "bail enforcement agent," and "personal surety agent" shall be defined as in Mississippi Code Section 83-39-1, *et seq*.

(i) Compliance Required. All agents and insurers shall comply fully with Mississippi Code Sections 83-39-1, *et seq*., and 99-5-1, *et seq*., and all related statutes and regulations.

Comment

Rule 8.1 provides definitions for use in Rule 8 and throughout these Rules, and replaces practice under former Rule 6.02 of the Uniform Rules of Circuit and County Court. The statutory provisions currently governing professional bail bond companies regulated by the Mississippi Commissioner of Insurance, as provided in Mississippi Code Section 83-39-1 *et seq*., are unaffected by Rule 8. This Rule is intended to complement existing statutory provisions governing bail matters in the courts, as provided in Mississippi Code Section 99-5-1 *et seq.* The forms required by Mississippi Code Sections 99-5-1 and 99-5-3 are unaffected.

A release on personal recognizance pursuant to section (a) is distinguishable from release conditioned on the posting of bond or other security.

Section (b) describes a type of bond not previously used in state court practice, but used extensively in federal criminal cases pursuant to 18 U.S.C. § 3142(b).

Sections (c) and (d) reflect current practice. *See* Miss. Code Ann. § 99-5-9. The form of a cash deposit bond previously prescribed by Rule 6.02(C.) of the Uniform Rules of Circuit and County Court is retained.

Section (f) clarifies the procedure when a person is arrested and permitted to post an appearance bond secured by sureties who may own equity in real property.

Sections (h) and (i) make clear that the statutory requirements and procedures related to professional bond companies and their bail bonds continue in full force.

Rule 8.2 Right to Pretrial Release on Personal Recognizance or on Bond.
(a) Right to Release. Any defendant charged with an offense bailable as a matter of right shall be released pending or during trial on the defendant's personal recognizance or on an appearance bond unless the court before which the charge is filed or pending determines that such a release will not reasonably assure the defendant's appearance as required, or that the defendant's being at large will pose a real and present danger to others or to the public at large. If such a determination is made, the court shall impose the least onerous condition(s) contained in Rule 8.4 that will reasonably assure the defendant's appearance or that will eliminate or minimize the risk of harm to others or to the

public at large. In making such a determination, the court shall take into account the following:

(1) the age, background and family ties, relationships and circumstances of the defendant;

(2) the defendant's reputation, character, and health;

(3) the defendant's prior criminal record, including prior releases on recognizance or on unsecured or secured appearance bonds, and other pending cases;

(4) the identity of responsible members of the community who will vouch for the defendant's reliability;

(5) violence or lack of violence in the alleged commission of the offense;

(6) the nature of the offense charged, the apparent probability of conviction, and the likely sentence, insofar as these factors are relevant to the risk of nonappearance;

(7) the type of weapon used (e.g., knife, pistol, shotgun, sawed-off shotgun, assault or automatic weapon, explosive device, etc.);

(8) threats made against victims or witnesses;

(9) the value of property taken during the alleged commission of the offense;

(10) whether the property allegedly taken was recovered or not, and damage or lack of damage to the property allegedly taken;

(11) residence of the defendant, including consideration of real property ownership, and length of residence in the defendant's domicile;

(12) in cases where the defendant is charged with a drug offense, evidence of selling or distribution activity that should indicate a substantial increase in the amount of bond;

(13) consideration of the defendant's employment status and history, the location of defendant's employment (e.g., whether employed in the county where the alleged offense occurred), and the defendant's financial condition;

(14) sentence enhancements, if any, included in the charging document; and

(15) any other fact or circumstance bearing on the risk of nonappearance or on the danger to others or to the public.

(b) Specific statutory limits apply. When a statute limits a judge's bail authority, such statutory limits shall apply to the extent any of the amounts listed in section (c) are in conflict therewith.

(c) Bond Guidelines. The following is established as a general guide for circuit, county, justice, and municipal courts in setting bail for persons charged with bailable offenses. Except in situations where release is required in the minimum scheduled amount pursuant to Rule 5.1(b) or (c), or any other Rule, courts may and should exercise discretion in setting bail above or below the scheduled amounts, as supported by consideration of the factors listed in Rule 8.2(a).

SECURED OR UNSECURED APPEARANCE BOND GUIDELINES
Recommended Range

FELONIES:

Capital felony $25,000 to No Bail Allowed

Manslaughter (or any other non-capital crime involving loss of human life)	$10,000 to $1,000,000
Drug Distribution and Trafficking	$ 5,000 to $1,000,000
All other non-capital felonies	
- punishable by maximum 20 years or more	$20,000 to $250,000
- punishable by maximum 10 years to 20 years	$10,000 to $100,000
- punishable by maximum up to 10 years	$ 5,000 to $50,000

MISDEMEANORS (not included elsewhere in the schedule):

- punishable by maximum 1 year	$500 to $2,000
- punishable by maximum 6 mos.	$250 to $1,000
- punishable by less than 6 mos.	$100 to $500
- punishable by fine only	$50 to Max. Fine/Costs*
Misdemeanor DUI and DWLS	$500 to $2,000
Municipal Ordinance Violations	$100 to $1,000

*Maximum amount of fine(s), court costs, and statutory assessments which might be due upon conviction.

Comment

Rule 8.2 embodies the guarantee against excessive bail provided by article 3, section 29, of the Mississippi Constitution, within the limitations stated therein. Rule 8.2 is based on the presumption of innocence of the accused, the constitutional right of a defendant charged with a noncapital offense to be released on bail, and the policy that a defendant should be released pending trial whenever possible. Under section (a), a defendant charged with an offense that is bailable as a matter of right is eligible for a personal recognizance release unless the judge determines that the defendant's presence would not be reasonably assured or that the defendant poses a real and present danger of harm to others. *See **United States v. Salerno**,* 481 U.S. 739, 107 S. Ct. 2095, 95 L. Ed. 2d 697 (1986) (upholding the constitutionality of pretrial detention based on dangerousness). Section (a) makes it possible to release on bail indigent defendants on non-financial conditions that make it reasonably likely that the defendant will appear. *See **Bandy v. United States**, 81 S. Ct. 197, 5 L. Ed. 2d 218 (1960) (questioning constitutionality of holding indigent defendant in custody for no reason other than the inability to raise money for bail).

Sections (a)(1) - (15) provide detailed guidance for the judge setting bond as to the range of inquiries that should be made prior to setting the conditions on, or the amount of, any personal recognizance or appearance bond. While no prior rule or statute required the inquiry described in section (a), such an inquiry has always been within the sound discretion and inherent power of a court setting terms of release. *See **Lee v. Lawson**, 375 So. 2d 1019, 1024 (Miss. 1979) (suggesting similar inquiry). Section (a) is intended to provide a helpful, non-exhaustive list for any court making such an inquiry, and is written to ensure that a judge not give inordinate weight to the nature of the present charge.

Section (b) provides that, in the event of a conflict with the amounts listed in (c), statutory limits on a judge's bail authority will control. *See, e.g.,* Miss. Code Ann. § 99-5-37 (defendant charged with certain domestic violence offenses).

While section (c) makes clear that the judge retains discretion to set any amount of bail above or below the suggested range, the bond guidelines set forth in section (c) should help reduce the disparities between courts who previously set bail without the guidance of a scheduled range. "Capital felony" is defined in Mississippi Code Section 1-3-4.

Rule 8.3 Release after Conviction and Sentencing.

A convicted defendant shall be entitled to bail pending appeal as prescribed by Mississippi Code Section 99-35-115. A condition of the appeal bond shall be that the defendant will obey every order and judgment of the Supreme Court or Court of Appeals or every order and judgment of the trial court affirmed by the Supreme Court or Court of Appeals. The sheriff shall not accept the appeal bond unless the appeal has been perfected. If a defendant is admitted to bail pending appeal, the trial court clerk shall so notify the clerk of the Supreme Court.

Comment

Rule 8.3 generally tracks former Rule 12.01 of the Uniform Rules of Circuit and County Court. Release after conviction and sentencing is governed by statute and uniform rule. *See, e.g.,* Rules 29 (Appeals from Justice or Municipal Court), 30 (Appeals from County Court), and M.R.A.P. 9 (Release in Criminal Cases).

Rule 8.4 Conditions of Release.

(a) Mandatory Conditions. Every order of release under this Rule shall contain the conditions that the defendant:

(1) appear in court, when required, and comply with all orders of the court;

(2) commit no crime;

(3) promptly notify the court of any change of address; and

(4) meet with your public defender or retained attorney, as directed.

(b) Additional Conditions. An order of release may include any one (1) or more of the following conditions reasonably necessary to secure a defendant's appearance or to protect the public:

(1) execution of an appearance bond in an amount specified by the court, either with or without requiring that the defendant deposit with the clerk security in an amount as required by the court;

(2) execution of a secured appearance bond;

(3) placing the defendant in the custody of a designated person or organization agreeing to supervise the defendant;

(4) restrictions on the defendant's travel, associations, or place of abode during the period of release;

(5) restrictions on the defendant's direct or indirect contact with any specified person(s);

(6) return to custody after specified hours;

(7) participation in, and successful completion of, any drug, alcohol, anger management, mental health, or other treatment required by the court, and/or substance testing;

(8) participation in General Educational Development (GED®) classes and testing or in any other educational activities required by the court;

(9) electronic monitoring; or

(10) any other conditions which the court deems reasonably necessary.

Comment

Rule 8.4 adds specific conditions of release drawn from portions of 18 U.S.C. § 3142(c) and from practice in various Mississippi courts in the exercise of their discretion and experience in such matters. Section (b)(10) vests the judge setting bond conditions with broad latitude to insure appearance of the defendant and protection of the public, and gives the judge flexibility in fashioning conditions of release.

Rule 8.5 Procedure for Determination of Release Conditions.

(a) Initial Decision. When a defendant is brought before a court for initial appearance, a determination of the conditions of release shall be made. The judge shall issue an order containing the conditions of release and shall inform the defendant of the conditions, the possible consequences of their violation, and that a warrant for the defendant's arrest may be issued immediately upon report of a violation.

(b) Amendment of Conditions. The court may, for good cause shown, on its own initiative or on application of either party, modify the conditions of release, after first giving the parties an adequate opportunity to respond to the proposed modification.

(c) Review by Circuit Court. No later than seven (7) days before the commencement of each term of circuit court in which criminal cases are adjudicated, the official(s) having custody of felony defendants being held for trial, grand jury action, or extradition within the county (or within the county's judicial districts in which the court term is to be held) shall provide the presiding judge, the district attorney, and the clerk of the circuit court the names of all defendants in their custody, the charge(s) upon which they are being held, and the date they were most recently taken into custody. The senior circuit judge, or such other judge as the senior circuit judge designates, shall review the conditions of release for every felony defendant who is eligible for bail and has been in jail for more than ninety (90) days.

Comment

Rule 8.5 establishes a mechanism for setting bail, and for periodically reviewing bail which has been set but has not been posted. These notice and review requirements should enhance the procedure for ensuring speedy trials or other timely dispositions of criminal cases, and should help avoid the possibility that a person in detention is overlooked by those having custody of that person.

The conditions of release will usually be set on the arrest warrant at the time of its issuance, pursuant to Rule 3.2(a). If not, or if the defendant cannot meet the conditions, the defendant will be afforded a release hearing at the initial appearance as provided by Rules 5.1 and 5.2. Thereafter, under section (b), the conditions can be modified, to be made either more or less stringent, depending on the circumstances. Section (c) is particularly important in requiring that the court and other interested personnel in the judicial system receive notice prior to each court term of the identities of those being held in custody, either without bail or without the ability to post bail. The clerk of the circuit court shall maintain the lists required by section (c). Section (c) also requires a review of the detention or bail status of those who have remained in custody for more than ninety (90) days.

Rule 8.6 Review of Conditions; Revocation of Bail.
(a) Issuance of Warrant. If it is alleged that a defendant previously released has committed a material breach of the conditions of release, then the court having jurisdiction over the defendant may procure the defendant's presence in court by issuing an order to appear before the court to show cause, or by issuing an arrest warrant under Rule 3.1. Such action shall be predicated upon a motion of the prosecuting attorney, or the court's own motion, which states with particularity:

(1) the facts or circumstances alleged to constitute a material breach of the conditions of release;

(2) that material misrepresentations or omissions of fact were made in securing the defendant's release; or

(3) that revocation is otherwise required by law.

If action is taken on motion of the prosecuting attorney, then a copy of the motion shall be served with the order or warrant, and a hearing shall be held on the motion without unnecessary delay.

(b) Hearing; Review of Conditions; Revocation of Release. If, after a hearing on the matters set forth in the motion, the court finds that the released defendant has materially breached the conditions of release, the court may modify the conditions or revoke the release. If a ground alleged for revocation of the release is that the defendant has committed a criminal offense or has made misrepresentations or omissions in informing the court of other charges pending against the defendant, the court may modify the conditions of release or revoke the release, if the court finds that there is probable cause to believe that the defendant committed the other pending offense(s).

(c) Cases Governed by Article 3, Section 29(2) of the Mississippi Constitution. In cases governed by Article 3, section 29(2) of the Mississippi Constitution of 1890, on motion of the prosecuting attorney or on the court's own motion, a court having jurisdiction over the defendant may revoke the defendant's bail.

Comment

Rule 8.6(a) permits either a warrant or a summons to be issued to take the person into custody for bail review or revocation proceedings. Section (c) is in accordance with article 3, section 29(2) of the Mississippi Constitution and governs situations where one previously admitted to bail for a felony has been charged with a new felony offense punishable by more than five (5) years of imprisonment. Upon finding probable cause for the new offense, either by the reviewing court or another court with jurisdiction (such as the court in which the new charge has been filed), this constitutional provision requires revocation of the prior bail and directs that the person will not be admitted to further bail. *See Dendy v. State*, 931 So. 2d 608, 614-15 (Miss. Ct. App. 2005), *cert. denied,* 933 So. 2d 303 (Miss. 2006).

Rule 8.7 Transfer and Disposition of Bond.
(a) Transfer Upon Supervening Indictment. An appearance bond or release order issued to assure the defendant's presence for proceedings following the filing of a charging affidavit shall automatically be transferred to the same, related, or lesser charge subsequently prosecuted by indictment unless, following indictment, the judge presiding, for good cause, shall order revocation or modification of the conditions of release, as provided in Rule 8.6(a) and (b).

(b) Filing and Custody of Appearance Bonds and Security. Appearance bonds and security shall be filed with the clerk of the court in which the case is pending. Whenever the case is transferred to another court, any appearance bond and security shall be transferred also.

(c) Surrender of Defendant by Surety. The surrender of the defendant by a surety shall be governed by Mississippi Code Sections 99-5-27 and 99-5-29. In the event that a Professional Bail Agent, Soliciting Bail Agent, or Insurer has provided a surety bond or other form of bail for a defendant without first obtaining payment in full for the premium on the bond, that defendant may not be surrendered because the defendant, or anyone assuming financial responsibility for the bond premium on the defendant's behalf, has failed to make any payment to the surety following release of the defendant.

(d) Forfeiture. If at any time it appears to the court that a defendant has failed to appear, the court shall proceed as appropriate pursuant to Mississippi Code Sections 99-5-25, 21-23-8, or 99-5-11, and any related statutes or regulations which may apply.

(e) Cancellation of Bond. At any time that the court finds there is no further need for an appearance bond, the court shall cancel the appearance bond and order the return of any security deposited with the clerk.

Comment

Rule 8.7(a) is consistent with current Mississippi practice regarding appearance bonds. The last sentence of section (c) addresses the situation where a bail bond company attempts to surrender the principal solely on the basis of nonpayment of the fee or commission, or any portion thereof, which was not collected at the time of issuance of the bond. Mississippi Code Section 83-39-25 plainly directs that the professional bail agent "shall charge and collect" the premium, commission, or fee due. However, if the bail agent nevertheless elects to contract with the principal to issue bail on the payment of less than the full amount due, any subsequent collection effort is merely a contractual matter which may be resolved in civil court, not in criminal court by means of incarceration for nonpayment. *See Brooks v. Pennington*, 995 So. 2d 733 (Miss. Ct. App. 2007). The statutes governing bail permit wide latitude to the surety to surrender a person on bail; however, nonpayment of a contractual obligation between the principal and professional bail agent is not, standing alone, a proper basis for surrender. Section (d) defers to the extensive statutory procedure governing forfeiture of bail bonds provided in Mississippi Code Sections 99-5-25, 21-23-8, and 99-5-11.

Rule 9 Trial Setting

(a) Trial Docket. Within sixty (60) days after arraignment (or waiver thereof), the court shall enter an order setting a date for trial. Trial shall be set for no later than two-hundred-and-seventy (270) days after arraignment (or waiver thereof). A docket of cases set for trial shall be maintained by the clerk or the court administrator. Cases set by the judge for trial must be ready at the appointed time.

(b) Criminal Docket to Have Priority. Insofar as is practicable, trials of criminal cases shall have priority over trials of civil cases.

(c) Continuance of Trial Date. For good cause shown, a continuance may be granted by written order of the court on its own motion, or on the motion of a party stating, with specificity, the reasons for the continuance.

Rule 10 Presence of Defendant, Witnesses, and Spectators

Rule 10.1 Right of Defendant to be Present; Waiver.
(a) Right to Be Present. The defendant has the right to be present at the arraignment and at every stage of the proceedings. A corporate criminal defendant may appear by counsel for all purposes at any proceeding.

(b) Waiver of the Right to Be Present.
(1) Except as provided in subsection (2), a defendant may waive the right to be present at any proceeding in the following manner:

> (A) with the consent of the court, by a knowing, intelligent, and explicit waiver in open court or by a written waiver executed by the defendant and by the defendant's attorney of record, filed in the case; or

(B) by the defendant's absence from any proceeding, if the court finds that such absence was voluntary and constitutes a knowing and intelligent waiver of the right to be present.

(2) A defendant may not waive the right to be present:

(A) during the imposition of his/her sentence in a felony case; or

(B) if the defendant is not represented by counsel, except in minor misdemeanor cases where the potential punishment is a fine only and carries no potential for the loss of liberty.

(c) Effect. If the defendant waives the right to be present, the trial may proceed to completion, including the return of the verdict.

(d) Unexcused Defendant. If a defendant is not present at the trial, or any stage of the proceedings, and the defendant's presence has not been waived or the absence has not been excused, the court, by order, may direct law enforcement officers forthwith to bring the defendant before the court.

Comment

The right of the defendant to be present protects various rights of the accused. *See* Miss. Const. art. 3, § 26 ("In all criminal prosecutions the accused shall have a right to be heard by himself or counsel, or both [and] to be confronted by the witnesses against him").

Section (b) allows a defendant to waive the right to be present, consistent with prior practice. The standards for waiver are those required for waiver of other constitutional rights. *See **Johnson v. Zerbst**,* 304 U.S. 458, 58 S. Ct. 1019, 82 L. Ed. 1461 (1938) ("an intentional relinquishment or abandonment of a known right or privilege").

The defendant may make an express waiver or the defendant may waive the right through voluntary absence from the proceeding. *See **Wales v. State**,*

73 So. 3d 1113 (Miss. 2011); *Taylor v. United States*, 414 U.S. 17, 94 S. Ct. 194, 38 L. Ed. 2d 174 (1973).

A defendant deemed to have waived the right to be present pursuant to subsection (b)(1)(B) might still be involuntarily absent and should be permitted to prove that fact in a subsequent or collateral proceeding. The decision to proceed in light of a voluntary waiver pursuant to subsection (b)(1)(B) is discretionary with the court. The court is in no instance required to proceed.

Rule 10.2 Consequences of Defendant's Disruptive Behavior.
(a) Disruptive Conduct. A defendant who engages in disruptive or disorderly conduct may be removed and shall forfeit the right to be present at that proceeding.

(b) Restoration of Right. The court shall grant any defendant so removed reasonable opportunities to return to the court upon the defendant's personal assurance of good behavior and/or such other conditions as the court may require. Any subsequent disruptive conduct on the part of the defendant may result in removal.

(c) Continuing Duty of Court. If feasible, the court shall employ reasonable means to enable a defendant removed from a proceeding under this Rule to hear, observe or be informed of the further course of the proceeding, and to consult with counsel at reasonable intervals.

Comment

Rule 10.2 is based upon *Illinois v. Allen*, 397 U.S. 337, 90 S. Ct. 1057, 25 L. Ed. 2d 353 (1970), *r'hg den.* 398 U.S. 915. Under Rule 10.2(a), a defendant, by disruptive conduct, may forfeit the right to be present, even in circumstances where the right could not be waived under Rule 10.1(b)(2). If the defendant is *pro se*, the court should consider appointing advisory counsel even if the defendant had refused to accept appointed counsel.

Section (c) is intended to encourage use of any practical audiovisual devices in communicating the progress of the proceeding to the defendant.

The court's contempt power also is applicable to such situations. *See* Rule 32.

Rule 10.3 Presence of Witnesses and Spectators.

(a) Witnesses. Pursuant to Rule 615 of the Mississippi Rules of Evidence, the court may, and at the request of either party shall, exclude prospective witnesses from the courtroom. The court also shall direct witnesses not to communicate with each other concerning the case until all have testified. If the court finds that a party's claim that a person is a prospective witness is not made in good faith, the person may be allowed to remain in the courtroom. Once a witness has testified on direct examination and has been made available to all parties for cross-examination and excused by the court, the witness shall be allowed to remain in the courtroom unless the court finds, upon application of a party or witness, that the presence of the witness would be prejudicial to a fair trial. This Rule does not authorize excluding a person whose presence a party shows to be essential to presenting the party's claim or defense.

(b) Spectators.
(1) Proceedings to be Open. All proceedings shall be open to the public unless the court finds, upon application of the defendant, that an open proceeding presents a danger to the defendant's right to a fair trial by an impartial jury.

(2) Exception for Certain Crimes. Pursuant to Article 3, Section 26 of the Mississippi Constitution, the court may exclude from the courtroom all persons except those necessary in the conduct of the trial.

(3) Victims. Pursuant to Article 3, Section 26A of the Mississippi Constitution, the alleged victim has the right to be present throughout all criminal proceedings when authorized by law. If the alleged victim is a witness, then Rule 10.3(a) controls.

(c) Removal. Any or all individuals may be removed from the courtroom for engaging in disorderly, disruptive, or contemptuous conduct, or when their conduct or presence constitutes a threat or menace to the court, parties, attorneys, witnesses, jurors, officials, members of the public, or a fair trial.

(d) Electronic Coverage of Proceedings. Electronic coverage of judicial proceedings shall be governed by the Mississippi Rules for Electronic and Photographic Coverage of Judicial Proceedings.

Comment

Rule 10.3(a) is consistent with Rule 615 of the Mississippi Rules of Evidence. The policy underlying the sequestration rule is that, by preventing a witness from hearing the testimony of another witness, the risk of fabrication, collusion, inaccuracy, and shaping of testimony is minimized. Because it is only at the designated phases where exclusion promotes the truth-finding process, prospective witnesses are permitted to attend during other phases, such as jury selection and legal argument. It is believed that the rule harmonizes the interest of a fair trial with the interest of witnesses in being personally present at the trial. The trial court retains discretion to exclude witnesses from the courtroom in those rare cases where it can be demonstrated that a fair trial cannot be held without such exclusion.

Rule 10.3(b)(1) sets forth the right of a defendant to a public trial as guaranteed by Article 3, Section 26, of the Mississippi Constitution, and subsection (b)(2) sets forth the exception for certain crimes contained therein. Rule 10.3(b)(3) embodies an alleged victim's right to be present set forth in Article 3, Section 26A, of the Mississippi Constitution and Mississippi Code Section 99-43-21. Mississippi Code Section 99-43-3(t) defines "victim" to mean "a person against whom the criminal offense has been committed, or if the person is deceased or incapacitated, the lawful representative." Mississippi Code Section 99-43-3(h) defines "criminal proceeding" as "a hearing, argument or other matter scheduled by and held before a trial court but does not include a lineup, grand jury proceeding or other matter not held in the presence of the court."

Section (c) gives the judge clear authority to clear the courtroom of any and all persons whose conduct is disruptive of the proceedings or whose presence poses a threat to others or to the proceedings.

Rule 11 Change of the Place of Trial

Rule 11.1 Change of Venue.

(a) Grounds. The trial judge, for good cause, may grant the defendant a change of venue. Good cause includes a satisfactory showing made to the court in writing, supported by the affidavits of two (2) or more credible persons, that the defendant cannot have a fair and impartial trial in the county where the offense is charged to have been committed.

(b) Prejudicial Pretrial Publicity. Whenever the grounds for change of venue are based on pretrial publicity, the trial judge shall consider the level of adverse publicity (both in extent of coverage and its inflammatory nature) and the potential effect of such publicity on the venire.

(c) Time for Filing Motion. A motion for change of venue should be made at the earliest opportunity after learning of the cause for challenge.

(d) Venue Upon Remand. When an action is remanded by an appellate court for a new trial or jury sentencing, all rights to request a change of venue may be asserted *de novo*.

Comment

Rule 11.1(a) is in accord with Article 3, Section 26 of the Mississippi Constitution, Mississippi Code Section 99-15-35, and former Rule 6.06 of the Uniform Rules of Circuit and County Court. If the request for a change of venue is based on pretrial publicity, section (b) requires the trial judge to consider the level of adverse publicity and its potential effect on the venire. *See McCune v. State*, 989 So. 2d 310, 317 n.14 (Miss. 2008).

Under section (d), an application for change of venue may be made when the matter is remanded by an appellate court for a new trial or jury sentencing. *See Maye v. State*, 49 So. 3d 1124, 1133 (Miss. 2010) (citing *State v. Caldwell*, 492 So. 2d 575, 577 (Miss. 1986)).

Rule 11.2 Transfer to Another County.

(a) Proceedings on Transfer. If a change of venue is granted pursuant to Rule 11.1, the judge shall direct that a certified copy of the order granting the change of venue be transmitted to the circuit clerk of the county to which the venue has been changed. The circuit clerk of the county to which the venue has been changed must file the certified order and designate a docket number for said case for future reference. Unless otherwise directed by the judge, all pleadings, motions, orders of the court, and other matters thereafter filed shall bear both the original number of the county of original venue and the assigned number of the county of changed venue, and shall be filed with the circuit clerk of the county of original venue. The judge may hear or determine all pretrial and post-trial matters in the county to which venue has been changed or in any county of the judge's district.

(b) Place of Trial. In all cases in which venue has been changed, it shall be within the judge's discretion, after the jury has been selected, to conduct the trial in the county of original venue or in the county to which venue has been transferred.

(c) Costs. All costs of a trial transferred from one county to another county, including the cost of transporting the jury from one county to another where the same is ordered, shall be borne by the county of original venue. The clerk of the county of original venue shall handle any appeal.

Comment

Rule 11.2 continues the practice under former Rule 6.06 of the Uniform Rules of Circuit and County Court, as well as prior statutory practice. *See* Miss. Code. Ann. §§ 99-15-37, 99-15-45.

Rule 12 Mental Examinations

Rule 12.1 Mental Competency; Definition.
(a) Mental Competency. There is a presumption of mental competency. In order to be deemed mentally competent, a defendant must have the ability to perceive and understand the nature of the proceedings, to communicate

rationally with the defendant's attorney about the case, to recall relevant facts, and to testify in the defendant's own defense, if appropriate. The presence of a mental illness, defect, or disability alone is not grounds for finding a defendant incompetent to stand trial. If as a result of mental illness, defect, or disability, a defendant lacks mental competency, then the defendant shall not be tried, convicted, or sentenced for a criminal offense.

(b) Mental Illness, Defect, or Disability. Mental illness, defect, or disability means a psychiatric or neurological disorder that is evidenced by behavioral or emotional symptoms, including congenital mental conditions, conditions resulting from injury or disease, or developmental disabilities.

Comment

"[T]he criminal trial of an incompetent defendant violates due process." *Cooper v. Oklahoma*, 517 U.S. 348, 354, 116 S. Ct. 1373, 1376, 134 L. Ed. 2d 498 (1996) (citation omitted). *See also Caylor v. State*, 437 So. 2d 444, 445 (Miss. 1983) (citing *Emanuel v. State*, 412 So. 2d 1187, 1188 (Miss. 1982)). The Mississippi Supreme Court has outlined the requisite abilities for a defendant to be deemed mentally competent. *See Jay v. State*, 25 So. 3d 257, 261 (Miss. 2009); *Martin v. State*, 871 So. 2d 693, 697-98 (Miss. 2004). In that analysis, there is a presumption of mental competency. *See Evans v. State*, 725 So. 2d 613, 660 (Miss. 1997). Rule 12.1 addresses only the defendant's competency to stand trial, and not the defendant's possible insanity at the time of the alleged offense. *See Parker v. State*, 30 So. 3d 1222, 1230-31 (Miss. 2010); *Medina v. California*, 505 U.S. 437, 448, 112 S. Ct. 2572, 2579, 120 L. Ed. 2d 353 (1992) ("there are significant differences between a claim of incompetence and a plea of not guilty by reason of insanity."); *Caylor*, 437 So. 2d at 447 n.1. If reasonable grounds exist to doubt the defendant's competence to stand trial, the procedures in Rules 12.2 through 12.6 should be followed.

Rule 12.2 Examination of Defendant's Mental Condition.
(a) Competency to Stand Trial or Be Sentenced. If at any time before or after indictment, the court, on its own motion or the motion of any party, has reasonable grounds to believe that the defendant is mentally incompetent, the court shall order the defendant to submit to a mental examination.

(b) Insanity Defense. If the defendant has timely raised a defense of insanity pursuant to Rule 17.4(b), the court, on its own motion or the motion of any party, may order the defendant to submit to a mental examination to investigate the defendant's mental condition at the time of the offense.

(c) Intellectual Disability in Death Penalty Cases. If at any time the court, on its own motion or the motion of any party, has reasonable grounds to believe that the defendant's intellectual disability bars imposition of a sentence of death, the court may order the defendant tested and/or examined to determine whether the defendant is intellectually disabled.

(d) Contents of Motion; Order. The motion shall state the facts upon which the mental examination is sought. The mental examination shall be conducted by a competent psychiatrist and/or psychologist approved by the court.

(e) Medical and Criminal History Records. All available medical and criminal history records shall be provided to the examining mental health expert as and when ordered by the court. A certificate of compliance shall be filed with the court documenting that the records were submitted as ordered.

Comment

Rule 12.2 includes standards provided in former Rules 9.06 and 9.07 of the Uniform Rules of Circuit and County Court. The determination of the defendant's mental competency should be made at the earliest practicable date. The United States Supreme Court has held that the failure to make a determination of competency when there are reasonable grounds to doubt such is fundamental constitutional error. *See **Drope v. Missouri***, 420 U.S. 162, 95 S. Ct. 896, 43 L. Ed. 2d 103 (1975); ***Pate v. Robinson***, 383 U.S. 375, 86 S. Ct. 836, 15 L. Ed. 2d 815 (1966). *See also **House v. State***, 754 So. 2d 1147, 1152 (Miss. 1999).

Sections (a) and (b) make clear that the determination of the defendant's competency to stand trial is separate and distinct from the determination of the defendant's sanity at the time of the offense. An examination to investigate competency may be combined with an examination to investigate the defendant's sanity at the time of the offense, provided that the judicial order makes a clear distinction between the two purposes for evaluation to ensure that the correct legal criteria are applied. While the test for competency is distinct, as a matter of law, from the test for sanity at the time of the offense, the reports prepared may contain information having a substantial bearing on both issues.

Section (c) extends this process to cases in which there are reasonable grounds to believe the defendant's intellectual disability precludes the imposition of a death sentence. *See* **Chase v. State**, 873 So. 2d 1013, 1027 (Miss. 2004) (citing **Atkins v. Virginia**, 536 U.S. 304, 122 S. Ct. 2242, 153 L. Ed. 2d 335 (2002)).

Rule 12.3 Appointment of Experts.
(a) Grounds for Appointment. If the court determines that reasonable grounds for a mental examination exist, it shall appoint a competent psychiatrist and/or psychologist to examine the defendant and, if necessary, to testify regarding the defendant's mental condition. The court has discretion to appoint more than one (1) examiner.

(b) Examination; Commitment. The court may order that a defendant be examined in an appropriate mental health facility, and it may commit a defendant to the Mississippi State Hospital or other appropriate mental health facility for no longer than reasonably necessary to conduct the examination if:

(1) the defendant cannot be examined on an outpatient basis;

(2) examination in an outpatient setting is unavailable; or

(3) commitment for examination is indispensable to a clinically valid diagnosis and report.

The examination and inpatient consultation shall be in the least restrictive appropriate setting.

(c) Reports.

(1) Opinion on Competency. A psychiatrist and/or psychologist appointed by the court pursuant to this Rule shall submit a report containing an opinion as to whether the defendant is competent, and the basis therefor. The report may also include additional findings and opinions concerning whether the defendant's mental condition creates a present danger to the defendant and/or others.

(2) Cause and Treatment of Incompetency. If the opinion referenced in (c)(1) is that the defendant is incompetent under the standards in Rule 12.1, the report shall also state the psychiatrist's and/or psychologist's opinion of:

(A) the condition causing the defendant's incompetency and the nature thereof;

(B) the treatment, if any, required for the defendant to attain competency;

(C) the most appropriate form and place of treatment, in view of the defendant's therapeutic needs and potential danger to the defendant and/or others, and an explanation of appropriate treatment alternatives;

(D) the likelihood of the defendant's attaining competency under treatment and the probable duration of the treatment; and

(E) the availability of the various types of acceptable treatment in the local geographic area, specifying the agencies or the settings in which the treatment might be obtained and whether the treatment would be available on an outpatient basis.

(3) Opinion on Mental Condition at Time of the Offense. In addition, if the court so orders, the report shall contain a statement of the psychiatrist's and/or psychologist's opinion of the following:

(A) the mental condition of the defendant at the time of the alleged offense;

(B) if the psychiatrist's and/or psychologist's opinion is that at the time of the alleged offense the defendant suffered from a mental disease or defect, the relation, if any, of such to the alleged offense, including:

(i) whether the defendant knew the nature and quality of the defendant's actions; and

(ii) if so, whether the defendant knew that the actions were wrong.

and

(C) such other matters as the court may deem appropriate.

(4) Opinion on Intellectual Disability in Death Penalty Cases. In addition, if the court so orders in a death penalty case, the report shall contain a statement of the psychiatrist's and/or psychologist's opinion as to whether the defendant is intellectually disabled and, if so, to what extent.

(d) Additional Expert Assistance. For good cause shown, the court may appoint additional experts and order the defendant to submit to physical, neurological, psychiatric, or psychological examinations, if necessary for an adequate determination of the defendant's mental condition.

(e) Costs. Any cost or expense in connection with the court-ordered mental examination(s) shall be paid by the county in which such criminal action originated.

Comment

Consistent with former Rule 9.06 of the Uniform Rules of Circuit and County Court and Mississippi Code Section 99-13-11, Rule 12.3(a) provides that where "reasonable grounds" exist, the court must appoint a competent psychiatrist and/or psychologist to examine the defendant and testify regarding the defendant's mental condition.

Section (b) ensures that a defendant will not be subjected to confinement in a mental health facility, unless a less restrictive alternative (such as local outpatient services) is unavailable, and it ensures that any confinement will be for only the minimum time required to conduct necessary examinations. *See Jackson v. Indiana*, 406 U.S. 715, 92 S. Ct. 1845, 32 L. Ed. 2d 435 (1972) (indefinite commitment based solely on incompetence to stand trial is unconstitutional). Once a court-ordered examination is completed, the examiner's report shall be filed with the court clerk, as provided in Rule 12.4.

Because the Rule 12.3 examination may also provide information concerning a possible insanity defense, the psychologist and/or psychiatrist may be required, pursuant to Rule 12.3(c)(3), to report on the mental condition of the defendant at the time of the alleged offense and on the relationship, if any, of the defendant's mental disease or defect to the alleged criminal act. Rule 12.3(c)(3) is not intended to establish a new legal test for insanity, or to change the test that was in use before adoption of these Rules. *See Nolan v. State*, 61 So. 3d 887, 895-97 (Miss. 2011) (citations omitted) ("Mississippi follows the *M'Naghten* standard for determining whether a defendant was sane at the time of the crime[,]" and has repeatedly declined to abandon that standard). Rule 12.3 merely requires the psychiatrist and/or psychologist to describe the defendant's mental condition in broad medical language. *See Roundtree v. State*, 568 So. 2d 1173 (Miss. 1990). Whether a person is mentally ill, and to what extent, is a medical judgment that a psychologist and/or psychiatrist should make; whether the defendant is sufficiently ill to be exonerated of criminal responsibility, i.e., whether the defendant is legally insane, is a legal judgment for the jury or trier of fact to make after proper instructions. Section (c)(4) extends these procedures to the question of the defendant's possible intellectual disability in death penalty cases. *See Chase v. State*, 873 So. 2d 1013, 1027 (Miss. 2004) (citing *Atkins v. Virginia*, 536 U.S. 304, 122 S. Ct. 2242, 153 L. Ed. 2d 335 (2002)).

Section (e) expressly provides for payment of the expenses of such professionals, within limits provided by law. *See* Miss. Code Ann. § 99-13-11. *Ake v. Oklahoma*, 470 U.S. 68, 105 S. Ct. 1087, 84 L. Ed. 2d 53 (1985), which holds that an indigent defendant is constitutionally entitled to a psychiatrist provided at state expense, is applicable when the defendant demonstrates to the trial judge that the defendant's sanity (or insanity) at the time of the offense is to be a significant factor at trial or that the defendant's mental state is likely to be a significant factor. Where a defense-consultant psychologist and/or psychiatrist is constitutionally required, such an expert may be appointed under Rule 12.3(a).

Rule 12.4 Disclosure of Mental Health Evidence; Reports of Appointed Experts.

(a) Generally. The reports of experts made pursuant to Rule 12.3 shall be submitted to the court clerk within ten (10) working days of the completion of the examination. All original reports shall be filed with the clerk, under seal. Upon receipt, the clerk shall copy and distribute the expert's report to the trial judge and to defense counsel. Defense counsel may redact any statements of the defendant (or summaries thereof) concerning the offense charged. A copy of the redacted report must be returned to the clerk within five (5) working days of its receipt and made available to the State. Any dispute regarding the extent of redaction shall be resolved by the trial judge.

(b) Mandatory Disclosure. If the defendant raises the affirmative defense of insanity, the State shall be furnished unredacted copies of the reports of experts made pursuant to Rule 12.3.

Comment

Under Rule 12.4, all expert reports produced pursuant to Rule 12 are to be disclosed to the court, to the defendant's attorney, and to the prosecuting attorney. Only one item of the report is excepted -- the defendant's statements concerning the actual offense charged. The United States Supreme Court has recognized that use of a defendant's statements during a court-ordered examination may compromise the defendant's right against self-incrimination. *See Estelle v. Smith*, 451 U.S. 454, 101 S. Ct. 1866, 68 L. Ed. 2d 359 (1981) (defendant's privilege against self-incrimination was violated when he was not advised of right to remain silent during court-ordered examination and prosecution introduced statements). *See also* MRE 503 cmt. ("No statement made by an accused in the course of an examination into competency to stand trial is admissible on the issue of guilt"). Thus, the prosecution may not make use of evidence obtained by compulsory mental examination of the defendant unless the defendant offers, either directly or through cross-examination, evidence in support of the affirmative defense of insanity. *See **Powell v. Texas**, 492 U.S. 680, 683-84, 109 S. Ct. 3146, 3149, 106 L. Ed. 2d 551 (1989) (defendant waives the privilege if the defendant introduces expert testimony on mental condition).

Rule 12.5 Hearing and Orders.

(a) Hearing. After submission of the reports, the court, upon its own motion or the motion of any party, shall promptly hold a hearing to determine the defendant's competency. The parties may introduce other evidence regarding the defendant's mental condition or, by stipulation (either written or stated on the record in open court), submit the matter on the experts' reports.

(b) Procedure. The competency hearing is a critical stage of the proceedings, at which the defendant shall be represented by counsel. The defendant shall be afforded an opportunity to testify, to present evidence, to subpoena witnesses, and to confront and cross-examine witnesses who appear at the hearing.

(c) Finding of Competence. If the court finds that the defendant is competent to stand trial, then the court shall make the finding a matter of record and order the case to proceed to trial.

(d) Finding of Incompetence. If the court finds that the defendant is incompetent to stand trial, then the court may commit the defendant to the Mississippi State Hospital, other appropriate mental health facility, or other place of treatment, either inpatient or outpatient, based on the report of a psychiatrist or psychologist pursuant to Rule 12.3(c)(2)(C) and (E). The order of commitment shall be filed with the court clerk and shall require that the defendant be examined by staff psychiatrist(s) and/or psychologist(s), and a written report be furnished to the court not less than every four (4) calendar months, stating:

(1) Whether there is a substantial probability that the defendant will become mentally competent to stand trial within the foreseeable future; and

(2) Whether progress toward competency is being made.

(e) Release from Commitment. If, within a reasonable time after entry of a commitment order, there is neither a determination that there is a substantial probability that the defendant will become mentally competent to stand trial nor progress toward competency, the court shall order that civil proceedings as provided in Mississippi Code Section 41-21-61, *et. seq.*, be instituted. Said proceedings shall advance notwithstanding that the defendant has criminal charges pending against him/her. The defendant shall remain in custody until determination of the civil proceedings.

Comment

Under Rule 12.5(a), upon the court's own motion or the motion of any party, a competency hearing shall be conducted. But in the absence of such motion, a hearing is permissible, but not mandatory. This represents a departure from practice under former Rule 9.06 of the Uniform Rules of Circuit and County Court.

Under section (d), if the court finds the defendant to be incompetent, it shall commit the defendant to an appropriate mental health facility or other place of treatment. No order made under this section is to be effective for longer than four (4) months, thereby insuring a frequent review of each incompetent defendant's status and progress. *See O'Connor v. Donaldson*, 422 U.S. 563, 575, 95 S. Ct. 2486, 2493, 45 L. Ed. 2d 396 (1975) ("even if . . . involuntary confinement was initially permissible, it could not constitutionally continue after that basis no longer existed"); *Jackson v. Indiana*, 406 U.S. 715, 720, 92 S. Ct. 1845, 1849, 32 L. Ed. 2d 435 (1972) (a state "cannot constitutionally commit [a] petitioner for an indefinite period simply on account of his incompetency to stand trial on the charges filed against him"). Sections (d) and (e) largely continue the procedure applicable under former Rule 9.06 of the Uniform Rules of Circuit and County Court.

Rule 12.6 Subsequent Hearings.

(a) Grounds. The court shall hold a hearing to assess the defendant's competency:

(1) on receiving a written report from a treating mental health professional stating that, in his/her opinion, the defendant has become competent to stand trial;

(2) on motion of either party, accompanied by the certificate of a mental health expert stating that, in the expert's opinion, the defendant is competent to stand trial; or

(3) on the court's own motion.

The parties may, by stipulation (either written or stated on the record in open court), submit the matter on the experts' reports.

(b) Finding of Competency. If the court finds that the defendant is competent to stand trial, the regular proceedings shall recommence without delay. The defendant shall be entitled to a rehearing of any proceeding if there are reasonable grounds to believe the defendant was prejudiced by the defendant's previous incompetency.

(c) Finding of Continuing Incompetency. If the court finds that the defendant remains incompetent, the court shall proceed in accordance with Rules 12.5(d) or (e).

Comment

Section (c) directs the court, upon finding that the defendant remains incompetent, to reconsider the alternatives presented in Rules 12.5(d) and (e). *Jackson v. Indiana*, 406 U.S. 715, 92 S. Ct. 1845, 32 L. Ed. 2d 435 (1972), held that the continuing commitment of a defendant must be justified by an appropriate showing by the state. Accordingly, the initial findings of the trial court are not relevant at this point, and questions regarding the continued incompetency of the defendant are to be considered by the trial court *de novo*.

Rule 13 The Grand Jury

Rule 13.1 Selection and Preparation of Grand Jurors.
(a) Summons. Grand jurors shall be summoned and impaneled as provided by law.

(b) Service of Grand Jury.
(1) Generally. Grand juries may be impaneled and serve both in term time and vacation.

(2) Number of Grand Jurors. The grand jury shall consist of at least fifteen (15) persons, but not more than twenty-five (25) persons, the exact number to be within the discretion of the judge impaneling the jury. If during the service of a grand jury the number of grand jurors able to serve on the grand jury shall become less than fifteen (15), then the circuit judge may have additional grand jurors summoned, impaneled, and charged in the same manner as the original grand jurors.

(3) Convening the Grand Jury. Upon impanelment, a grand jury may be convened and reconvened by order of the court. The grand jury will continue to serve until the next grand jury is impaneled and it may return indictments to court in term time or vacation notwithstanding intervening terms of court between the time the grand jury is impaneled and the time an indictment is returned.

(c) Impanelment of Grand Jury. Before swearing grand jurors as such, the grand jurors shall be examined by the court, on oath, touching their qualifications. After the grand jurors have been sworn and impaneled, no objection shall be raised, by plea or otherwise, to the grand jury, but the impaneling of the grand jury shall be conclusive evidence of its competency and qualifications. However, any party interested may challenge or except to the array for fraud.

Comment

"Historically and at present, a grand jury is an independent body empowered with the authority to investigate potential crimes and, if probable cause is found, to indict for criminal offenses." *Entergy Mississippi, Inc. v. State*, 132 So. 3d 568, 572 (Miss. 2014).

Rule 13.1 follows former Rule 7.02 of the Uniform Rules of Circuit and County Court, and incorporates the procedure for summoning and impaneling grand juries provided in Mississippi Code Section 13-5-1, *et. seq. See* Miss. Const. art. 14, § 264 ("The Legislature shall, by law, provide for the qualifications of grand and petit jurors. The Legislature shall provide, by law, for procuring a list of persons so qualified, and the drawing therefrom of grand and petit jurors"). Rule 13.1(c) tracks the language in Mississippi Code Section 13-5-43.

Rule 13.2 Instructions, Duties, and Powers of Grand Jury.
(a) Charge to the Grand Jury.
(1) By Whom. Only the circuit judge may deliver the charge to the grand jury, except that the circuit clerk or deputy court clerk may read the charge as proposed by the circuit judge when the judge shall be unable to deliver the charge by reason of physical infirmity.

(2) Charge. The circuit judge shall charge the grand jury according to the matters required by law as the judge deems fit and proper. A sample charge which may be used is attached as an Appendix to these Rules.

(b) Examination of County Records. The grand jury shall have free access at all proper hours to the papers, records, accounts and books of all county officers for all examinations which it may see fit to make, and may make report to the court in relation thereto.

Comment

Rule 13.2(a) is largely derived from former Rule 7.01 of the Uniform Rules of Circuit and County Court. Rule 13.2(b) incorporates the provisions of Mississippi Code Section 13-5-57. *See also Entergy Mississippi, Inc. v. State*, 132 So. 3d 568, 572 (Miss. 2014) (quoting *Ex parte Jones County Grand Jury, First Judicial Dist.*, 705 So. 2d 1308, 1315 (Miss. 1997)) ("Grand juries have 'broad investigative power and wide latitude in conducting an investigation'").

Rule 13.3 Grand Jury Foreperson.
(a) Selection of Foreperson; Oath.

(1) Foreperson. The court shall appoint a foreperson of the grand jury to whom the following oath shall be administered in open court, in the presence of the other grand jurors:

> You, as foreperson of this grand inquest, shall diligently inquire into, and true presentment make, of all such matters and things as shall be given you in charge, or otherwise come to your knowledge, touching the present service. The counsel of the state, your fellows, and your own you will keep secret. You shall not present any person through malice, hatred or ill will, nor shall you leave any person unpresented through fear, favor or affection, or for any reward, hope or promise thereof, but in all your presentments, you shall present the truth, the whole truth, and nothing but the truth, to the best of your skill and understanding. So help you God.

(2) Oath of Other Grand Jurors. The following oath shall be administered to the other grand jurors:

> The same oath that your foreperson has now taken before you on the foreperson's part, you, and each of you, shall well and truly observe, and keep on your respective parts. So help you God.

(3) Replacement of Foreperson. If a foreperson becomes unable to continue service as a grand juror, the court shall appoint another member of the grand

jury as replacement. The fact that the original foreperson was replaced shall not be grounds for attacking the validity of the acts or indictments of the grand jury.

(b) Powers and Duties of Foreperson. The foreperson is empowered to preside over the grand jury proceedings, issue or cause to be issued subpoenas (*ad testificandum* and *duces tecum*), and swear all witnesses. A record shall be kept by the foreperson and returned to court, certified and signed by the foreperson, of the names of all witnesses sworn before the grand jury. The foreperson shall also submit a written report of the proceedings of the grand jury to the court or clerk; endorse any indictment returned by the grand jury as a "True Bill" and sign the foreperson's name thereto; and return a "No True Bill" list to the circuit clerk, to be kept under seal, although the clerk is allowed to disclose to a defendant that his/her case has received a "No True Bill."

Comment

Rule 13.3 is based, in part, on former Rule 7.02 of the Uniform Rules of Circuit and County Court. The oaths in this Rule are taken from Mississippi Code Section 13-5-45. Such oaths may be administered to all grand jurors at the same time. The powers and duties of the foreperson are derived from Mississippi Code Section 13-5-63 and *Entergy Mississippi, Inc. v. State*, 132 So. 3d 568, 574 (Miss. 2014). They should be included in the charge to the grand jury.

Rule 13.4 Recalcitrant Witnesses; Contempt.
(a) Recalcitrant Witnesses. When a witness under examination before the grand jury refuses to testify, to answer a question or to give evidence, the foreperson and/or the district attorney shall present to the court the question or evidence requested and the refusal of the witness. If, after inquiry, the court decides that the witness is bound to testify, answer, or give the evidence, the court shall so inform the witness. If the witness persists in refusing to testify, answer the question, or give evidence, the court shall proceed with the witness as in cases of similar refusal in other judicial proceedings.

(b) Request for Contempt Proceedings. The foreperson and/or the district attorney may request the court to initiate a contempt proceeding against any person whose conduct violates these Rules or disrupts the grand jury proceedings.

Comment

Rule 13.4(a) is derived from former Rule 7.05 of the Uniform Rules of Circuit and County Court. Rule 13.4(b) authorizes the foreperson and/or the district attorney to request the court to employ its enforcement powers to secure compliance with these Rules through a contempt proceeding under Rule 32.3.

Rule 13.5 Persons Authorized to be Present During Sessions of the Grand Jury; Grand Jury Secrecy.

(a) Persons Authorized to be Present. No person other than the grand jurors, the witness under examination, prosecutors authorized to present evidence, and the interpreter, if any, shall be present during sessions of the grand jury. No person other than the grand jurors shall be present during their deliberation and voting.

(b) Grand Jury Secrecy.

(1) Generally. A grand juror, except when called as a witness in court, shall keep secret the proceedings and actions taken in reference to matters brought before the grand jury for six (6) months after final adjournment of the grand jury, and the name and testimony of any witness appearing before the grand jury shall be kept secret.

(2) Announcements Concerning Deliberations Prohibited. No attorney general, district attorney, county attorney, other prosecuting attorney, or other officer of the court shall announce to any unauthorized person what the grand jury will consider in its deliberations. If such information is disclosed, the disclosing person may be found in contempt of court punishable by fine or imprisonment.

(3) Disclosure of Indictments Prohibited. No grand juror, witness, attorney general, district attorney, county attorney, other prosecuting attorney, clerk, sheriff or other officer of the court shall disclose to any unauthorized person that an indictment is being found or returned into court against a defendant or disclose any action or proceeding in relation to the indictment before the finding

of an indictment, within six (6) months thereafter, or before the defendant is arrested or gives bail or recognizance.

Comment

Rule 13.5(b) preserves former Rule 7.04 of the Uniform Rules of Circuit and County Court and Mississippi Code Section 13-5-61. Rule 13.5(b)(2) authorizes the court to employ its contempt powers pursuant to Rule 32.3 to punish unauthorized disclosure of grand jury deliberations. *See* Miss. Code Ann. § 13-5-61. Rule 13.5(b)(3) does not preclude a prosecutor from informing a victim on the status of a charge, pursuant to Mississippi Code Section 99-7-9.

Rule 13.6   Grand Jury Proceedings.

(a) Number of Grand Jurors Necessary to Indict; Grand Jury Not To Do Certain Things. A grand jury has the power to indict any person upon affirmative vote of twelve (12) or more grand jurors. The grand jury report should not accuse any person by name of an offense, malfeasance, or misfeasance unless an indictment is returned. If accusations are included in a grand jury report, the comments may be expunged upon the motion of the individual or on motion of the court.

(b) Return of Indictment. When an indictment is found, it must be endorsed "A True Bill," shall be signed by the foreperson, and may be signed by one of the prosecuting attorneys.

(c) Presentment of Indictments and Grand Jury Reports. All indictments and grand jury reports must be presented to the clerk of the circuit court by the foreperson or the foreperson's designee, must be endorsed with the foreperson's name, and must be accompanied by the foreperson's affidavit that all indictments were concurred in by twelve (12) or more members of the grand jury and that at least fifteen (15) grand jurors were present during all deliberations. Indictments and grand jury reports must be marked "filed," and such entries must be dated and signed by the clerk. Unless the party indicted is in custody or on bond or recognizance, entry of the indictment shall be by number only, and no publicity may be given to the existence of the indictment. An arrest warrant (capias) for the person indicted shall immediately issue and be served. After the arrest of the person indicted, and before arraignment, a copy of the indictment shall be served on such person.

(d) Notice of Indictment. If the defendant has previously been released on bond or recognizance, or had an initial appearance under Rule 5.2, the court or the circuit clerk may notify the defendant, defendant's counsel, and/or defendant's bondsperson of the indictment in lieu of arrest.

(e) Failure to Return an Indictment. If the grand jury fails to return an indictment on a charge presented to it, the foreperson shall promptly so report to the court in writing. Unless the court shall order otherwise, the defendant:

(1) if held in custody, shall be released forthwith; or

(2) if previously conditionally released, shall be relieved of any obligation made in connection with such conditional release, along with the surety.

Comment

Rule 13.6(a) preserves former Rule 7.03 of the Uniform Rules of Circuit and County Court. *See also* Miss. Code Ann. § 99-7-11. Rule 13.6(c) largely embodies the statutory requirements contained in Mississippi Code Section 99-7-9.

Rule 13.7 Appearance of Persons Under Investigation; Immunity and Privilege.

(a) Appearance. A person under investigation by the grand jury may be invited or compelled to appear before the grand jury or, upon that person's written request, may be permitted by the grand jury to appear. Unless immunity has been granted to the person under investigation as provided in section (b), he/she shall be advised:

(1) of the right to remain silent, that anything he/she says may be used against him/her in a court of law;

(2) that he/she has the right to consult in private with an attorney outside the grand jury room at reasonable intervals while giving testimony;

(3) that, if he/she is unable to employ counsel because of indigency as defined in Rule 7.3, the court will appoint an attorney to represent him/her, and

(4) that he/she may at any time stop giving testimony and refuse to answer further questions.

(b) Immunity and Privilege. In any investigation before a grand jury, the prosecuting attorney may present, for court approval, a written agreement for a person under investigation to be granted immunity from prosecution for the offense(s) under investigation and any related or lesser-included offense(s) thereof.

Comment

Rule 13.7(a) permits a person under investigation by the grand jury to appear before that body by written request. *See* **United States v. Levinson**, 405 F. 2d 971, 980 (6th Cir. 1968), *cert. denied*, 395 U.S. 958, 89 S. Ct. 2097, 23 L. Ed. 2d 744 (1969) ("One accused of crime may oftentimes, by himself testifying before the grand jury, clear up the charges against him so that no indictment is returned"). The rule is discretionary, and does not create an absolute right on the part of a person under investigation to appear before the grand jury. Federal courts have long held that a potential defendant has no absolute right to appear before a grand jury. *See, e.g.,* **Duke v. United States**, 90 F. 2d 840, 841 (4th Cir. 1937), *cert. denied*, 302 U.S. 685, 58 S. Ct. 33, 82 L. Ed. 528 (1937) ("There is no right on the part of one whose conduct is being investigated by a grand jury to petition the grand jury or to appear before it, which is guaranteed by the Constitution or otherwise"). Consistent with practice in federal courts, a person under investigation is given the right to consult with an attorney outside the grand jury room, as a means of safeguarding the right against self-incrimination. *See, e.g.,* **United States v. Corallo**, 413 F. 2d 1306, 1329-30 (2d Cir. 1969), *cert. denied*, 396 U.S. 958, 90 S. Ct. 431, 24 L. Ed. 2d 422 (1969).

Section (b) provides that the prosecuting attorney shall furnish any immunity agreement to the court, in writing, for approval. *See* Miss. Code Ann. § 99-15-53; ***Wright v. McAdory***, 536 So. 2d 897, 899 (Miss. 1988) (enforceability of immunity agreement predicated upon obtaining "approval of the circuit court"). Transactional immunity is extended to the person under investigation in such circumstances. *See **Wright***, 536 So. 2d at 904-05 ("we hold that Article 3, Section 26 of the Mississippi Constitution requires a transactional immunity grant[,]," as "[o]nly such broad immunity will make the individual as secure as if he had remained silent"; the lone exception pertains to perjury); ***Kellum v. State***, 194 So. 2d 492, 493 (Miss. 1967) ("Witnesses who voluntarily appear before grand juries and other investigative bodies have a constitutional right not to be required to testify against themselves"); ***State v. Milam***, 210 Miss. 13, 48 So. 2d 594, 596 (1950) ("It is well settled in Mississippi and elsewhere that the constitutional privilege against self-incrimination applies to proceedings before a grand jury").

A person under investigation granted immunity may not refuse to testify based on the privilege against self-incrimination. *See **Wright***, 536 So. 2d at 903-04. The enforcement of this duty to testify is pursuant to the court's contempt powers under Rule 32.

Rule 14 Indictment

Rule 14.1 Nature and Contents.
(a) Contents Generally.
(1) Elements and Notice. The indictment upon which the defendant is to be tried shall be a plain, concise and definite written statement of the essential facts and elements constituting the offense charged and shall fully notify the defendant of the nature and cause of the accusation. Formal and technical words are not necessary in an indictment, if the offense can be substantially described without them.

(2) Other Matters. An indictment shall also include the following:

(A) the name of the accused;

(B) the date on which the indictment was filed in court;

(C) a statement that the prosecution is brought in the name and by the authority of the State of Mississippi;

(D) the county and, in two-district counties, the judicial district in which the indictment is brought;

(E) the date and, if applicable, the time at which the offense was alleged to have been committed;

(F) the signature of the foreperson of the grand jury issuing it; and

(G) the words "against the peace and dignity of the state."

(3) Surplusage. The court, upon motion, may strike from the indictment any surplusage, including unnecessary allegations or aliases.

(b) Enhanced Punishment for Subsequent Offenses. When an indictee may be eligible for enhanced punishment because of one (1) or more prior convictions, the State shall either:

(1) specify such prior conviction(s) in the indictment, identifying each such prior conviction by the name of the crime, the name of the court in which each such conviction occurred and the cause number(s), the date(s) of conviction, and, if relevant, the length of time the accused was incarcerated for each such conviction; or

(2) after indictment, and at least thirty (30) days before trial or entry of a plea of guilty, file with the court formal notice of such prior conviction(s). The notice shall be served upon the defendant or the defendant's attorney and shall contain the same information specified in subsection (1) of this rule. An untimely-filed formal

notice is permitted only when the thirty (30) day requirement is expressly waived, in writing, by the defendant. Clerical mistakes in such formal notice may, with leave of the court, be amended prior to the pronouncement of sentence.

(c) Charging the Offense. The indictment shall state for each count the citation of the statute or other provision of law which the defendant is alleged to have violated.

(d) Incorporation by Reference. A count may incorporate by reference facts alleged in a previous count.

(e) Notice of Necessarily Included Offenses. Specification of an offense in an indictment shall constitute notice of a charge of that offense and of all lesser offenses included therein.

(f) Admonishment. The indictment shall neither be shown to the jury, admitted into evidence, nor sent into the jury room.

Comment

Rule 14.1(a) is based upon former Rule 7.06 of the Uniform Rules of Circuit and County Court. The rule now provides that, in addition to the essential facts constituting the offense charged, the indictment must also include the essential elements of the offense charged. This includes all facts and elements necessary to enhance a sentence that are required to be found by a jury. *See Apprendi v. United States*, 530 U.S. 466, 490, 120 S. Ct. 2348, 2362-63, 147 L. Ed. 2d 435 (2000) ("Other than the fact of a prior conviction, any fact that increases the penalty for a crime beyond the prescribed statutory maximum must be submitted to the jury, and proved beyond a reasonable doubt"). *See, e.g.*, Miss. Code Ann. § 41-29-142 (providing an enhanced penalty for drug crimes that occur in close proximity to a school, church, public park, etc.).

Ten (10) counties contain two (2) judicial districts. Rule 14.1(a)(2)(D) requires the indictment to state whether it is brought in the first or second judicial district of that county.

Rule 14.1(b) builds on practice under former Rule 11.03 of the Uniform Rules of Circuit and County Court. Prior conviction(s) utilized to enhance punishment shall be included in either the indictment or a formal notice filed at least thirty (30) days before trial or the entry of a guilty plea, absent written waiver of the thirty (30) day requirement by the defendant.

Rule 14.1(e) provides that allegations of facts constituting an offense will also encompass all lesser offenses, without the need for an explicit statement to that effect. *See Downs v. State*, 962 So. 2d 1255 (Miss. 2007); *Porter v. State*, 616 So. 2d 899 (Miss. 1993).

Rule 14.2 Multi-Count Indictments; Joinder of Defendants.
(a) Joinder of Offenses. The indictment may charge a defendant in separate counts with two (2) or more offenses triable in the same court if the offenses charged – whether felonies, misdemeanors or both – are:

(1) based on the same act or transaction; or

(2) connected with or constitute parts of a common scheme or plan.

(b) Joinder of Defendants. Two (2) or more defendants may be charged in the same indictment upon which they are to be tried when:

(1) Each defendant is charged with accountability for each offense charged;

(2) Each defendant is charged with conspiracy and some of the defendants are also charged with one (1) or more offenses alleged to have been committed in furtherance of the conspiracy; or

(3) All defendants are not charged in each count, but it is alleged that the several offenses charged were part of a common scheme or plan.

(c) Trial of Joined Offenses.

(1) Where two (2) or more offenses are properly charged in separate counts of a single indictment, all such charges may be tried in a single proceeding.

(2) The trier of fact shall return a separate verdict for each count of an indictment drawn under section (a).

(d) Sentencing. When a defendant is convicted of two (2) or more offenses charged in separate counts of an indictment, the court shall impose separate sentences for each such conviction. Nothing contained in this Rule, however, shall be construed to prohibit the court from exercising its authority to suspend either the imposition or execution of any sentence(s) or to prohibit the court from exercising its discretion to impose such sentences to run either concurrently with or consecutively to each other or to any other sentence(s) previously imposed upon the defendant.

Comment

Rule 14.2 largely continues prior practice under former Rules 7.07 and 7.08 of the Uniform Rules of Circuit and County Court.

Rule 14.3 Severance.
(a) Severance Generally.
(1) Severance in Death Penalty Cases. The court shall order a severance of defendants in cases in which the State seeks the death penalty.

(2) Severance in Non-Death Penalty Cases. The court may, on motion of the state or a defendant, grant a severance of defendants or offenses if it is deemed appropriate to promote the fair determination of a defendant's guilt or innocence of each offense.

(b) Timeliness and Waiver. A defendant's motion to sever offenses and/or defendants must be made at the earliest opportunity. The right to move for severance may be deemed to have been waived if a proper motion is not timely made.

(c) Severance during Trial. No severance of offenses or defendants may be ordered after trial has commenced unless the defendant consents or a mistrial has properly been declared as to such offense or defendant. Severance of offense(s) during trial, upon motion of the defendant or with the defendant's consent, shall not bar a subsequent trial of that defendant on the offense(s) severed.

Comment

When deciding whether severance is appropriate, "the trial court should consider the following factors: (1) the time period between the offenses, (2) whether the evidence proving each count would be admissible to prove each of the other counts, and (3) whether the crimes are interwoven." ***Richardson v. State***, 74 So. 3d 317, 324 (Miss. 2011) (citation omitted).

Rule 14.4 Amendment of Indictments; Defects in Indictments.

(a) Amendment of Indictments. For good cause shown, indictments may be amended as to form but not as to the substance of the offense charged. Amendment may be allowed only if the defendant is afforded a fair opportunity to present a defense and is not unfairly surprised.

(b) Raising Defect in Indictment. Defects respecting the indictment shall be raised by written motion.

Comment

"No person shall be held to answer for a capital, or otherwise infamous crime, unless on a presentment or indictment of a Grand Jury. . . ." U.S. Const. amend. V. *See also* Miss. Const. art. 3, § 27.

Rule 14.4(a) allows an indictment to be amended as to form only upon a showing of good cause.

Under Rule 14.4(b), issues previously raised by demurrer or motion to quash the indictment may be brought in a motion to dismiss. *See* Miss. Code Ann. §§ 99-7-21, 99-7-23. A motion to dismiss the indictment also may be based upon objections to the composition of the grand jury, the legal insufficiency of, or a defect in, the indictment, or the failure of the indictment to charge an offense.

Rule 14.5 Waiver of Indictment; Proceeding by Information. No person shall, for any felony, be proceeded against without indictment, except by means of an information where a defendant represented by counsel waives indictment by sworn statement in writing.

Comment

Rule 14.5 is consistent with Article 3, Section 27 of the Mississippi Constitution. A properly executed waiver of indictment vests the trial court with full authority to dispose of the felony offense for which indictment was waived. *See Williams v. State*, 708 So. 2d 1358, 1364 (Miss. 1998).

Rule 14.6 Dismissal.
(a) By the Prosecutor. The prosecuting attorney may, with leave of the court having jurisdiction, dismiss an indictment or any count thereof.

(b) Unnecessary Delay. The court may dismiss an indictment or any count thereof, if unnecessary delay occurs in bringing a defendant to trial.

(c) Effect of Dismissal. Dismissal of a prosecution shall be without prejudice to the commencement of another prosecution, unless the court orders that the interests of justice require that the dismissal be with prejudice.

(d) Release of Defendant; Discharge of Bond. When a prosecution is dismissed, the defendant shall be released from custody, unless the defendant is in custody on some other charge, and any bail shall be released and held for naught and/or sureties discharged, or money deposited in lieu thereof shall be refunded.

Comment

Rule 14.6(a) and (b) are derived from Federal Rule of Criminal Procedure 48. Rule 14.6(a) requires the prosecuting attorney to seek permission of the court to dismiss a prosecution, which is consistent with Mississippi Code

Section 99-15-53. Rule 14.6(b) recognizes the court retains some discretion in determining what constitutes unnecessary delay.

Under Rule 14.6(c), the dismissal of a charge is without prejudice unless the court so specifies. *See Conwill v. State*, 94 So. 3d 1173, 1176 (Miss. Ct. App. 2011); *Beckwith v. State*, 615 So. 2d 1134, 1147 (Miss. 1992).

Rule 15 Arraignment and Pleas

Rule 15.1 Necessity of Arraignment.
(a) Service of Indictment. Before arraignment, a copy of the indictment shall be served on the defendant. Arraignment, unless waived by the defendant, shall be held within thirty (30) days after the defendant is served with the indictment. When arraignment cannot be held within the time specified because the defendant is in custody elsewhere, it shall be held as soon as possible.

(b) In General. An arraignment, unless waived, shall be conducted in open court and must consist of:

(1) ensuring that the defendant has a copy of the indictment;

(2) reading the indictment to the defendant or stating to the defendant the substance of the charge;

(3) asking the defendant to plead to the indictment;

(4) determining whether the defendant is represented by counsel and, if not, appointing counsel, if appropriate, under Rule 7;

(5) reviewing the bond previously set, if appropriate; and

(6) setting reasonable deadlines for the filing and hearing of all pretrial motions. Pretrial motions shall include, but are not limited to, motions: to dismiss, to suppress evidence, to request discovery,

for continuance, for severance, for appointment of experts, for mental examination, or for any other matters which may delay the trial.

(c) Waiving Reading of Indictment. Reading of the indictment may be waived if the defendant is represented and attended by counsel.

(d) Waiving Appearance. A defendant need not be present for the arraignment if the defendant, in a written waiver signed by both the defendant and the defendant's attorney, has waived appearance and has affirmed that the defendant received a copy of the indictment and that the plea is not guilty.

(e) Video Conferencing. Video conferencing may be used to arraign a defendant pursuant to Rule 1.8.

(f) Codefendants. Defendants who are jointly charged may be arraigned separately or jointly. If codefendants are arraigned at the same time and charged with the same offense, the indictments need be read only once, with stated identification of each defendant.

(g) Waiving Arraignment. Arraignment is deemed waived when the defendant proceeds to trial or enters a guilty plea without objection.

Comment

Rule 15.1 is largely derived from former Rules 8.01 and 8.02 of the Uniform Rules of Circuit and County Court. Section (a) requires that, whenever possible, arraignment be held within thirty (30) days after service of the indictment. The date of arraignment is an important point of reference for setting the date of trial under Rule 9(a) which, like former Rule 8.01 of the Uniform Rules of Circuit and County Court, provides that "[w]ithin sixty (60) days after arraignment (or waiver thereof), the court shall enter an order setting a date for trial. Trial shall be set for no later than two-hundred-seventy (270) days after arraignment (or waiver thereof)."

Section (b) is basically a checklist for the court and counsel in conducting an arraignment. Many of the items traditionally covered at the arraignment are included in the initial appearance. *See* Rule 5.2. They need not be repeated.

Section (d) permits the defendant to waive the right to appear at arraignment. It appears that the formal in-court taking of a plea of not guilty should not be required so long as the rights of the defendant are protected and an adequate record is made. Thus, the rule permits formal arraignment to be bypassed if the defendant is assisted by counsel and files a written waiver of arraignment and a plea of not guilty that also acknowledges receipt of a copy of the charge against the defendant.

Section (e) permits video conferencing of an arraignment pursuant to Rule 1.8.

Rule 15.2 Proceedings at Arraignment.
(a) Pleas. A defendant may plead not guilty, guilty, or, with leave of the court in misdemeanor cases, *nolo contendere*.

(b) Failure or Refusal to Plead. If the defendant, on arraignment, refuses or neglects to plead, stands mute, or pleads evasively, the court will enter a plea of not guilty and will set the case for trial.

(c) Absence of Defendant. If the defendant is released on bail or recognizance, and does not appear to be arraigned, or as required by the bond or recognizance, the court may, in addition to forfeiture of bail, direct the clerk to issue a bench warrant to bring the defendant before the court.

Comment
Rule 15.2 is largely based upon former Rules 8.03 and 8.04 of the Uniform Rules of Circuit and County Court. *See also* Miss. Code Ann. § 99-15-23.

The pleas enumerated in Rule 15.2(a) embrace the use of "best interest" or *Alford* pleas. *See Sims v. State*, 134 So. 3d 300, 302 n.3 (quoting *North*

Carolina v. Alford, 400 U.S. 25, 37, 91 S. Ct. 160, 27 L. Ed. 2d 162 (1970)) ("under a 'best interest plea,' the accused 'may voluntarily, knowingly, and understandingly consent to the imposition of a prison sentence even if he is unwilling or unable to admit his participation in the acts constituting the crime'"). But *Alford* added that:

> [b]ecause of the importance of protecting the innocent and of insuring that guilty pleas are a product of free and intelligent choice, various state and federal court decisions properly caution that pleas coupled with claims of innocence should not be accepted unless there is a factual basis for the plea, . . . and until the judge taking the plea has inquired into and sought to resolve the conflict between the waiver of trial and the claim of innocence.

Alford, 400 U.S. at 38 n.10 (internal citations omitted). Rule 15.3(c) requires that "[b]efore the trial court may accept a plea of guilty, the court must determine that the plea is voluntarily and intelligently made and that there is a factual basis for the plea."

In Mississippi, *nolo contendere* pleas are unavailable in felony cases. *See Welch v. State*, 958 So. 2d 1288, 1289 (Miss. Ct. App. 2007); *Bush v. State*, 922 So. 2d 802, 805 (Miss. Ct. App. 2005); *Keyes v. State*, 312 So. 2d 7, 10 (Miss. 1975) (citing *Bruno v. Cook*, 224 So. 2d 567 (Miss. 1969)) ("the plea of *nolo contendere* is only available in light or petty misdemeanor cases, not in felony cases"); Miss. Code Ann. § 21-23-7(8). The entry of a *nolo contendere* plea also requires leave of the court. *See Williams v. State*, 130 Miss. 827, 94 So. 882, 884 (1923) (quoting 1 Bishop's New Criminal Procedure, § 802) (*nolo contendere* "is pleadable only by leave of court").

Rule 15.3 Entry of Plea of Guilty or *Nolo Contendere*.
(a) Defendant's Presence at Plea.
(1) Defendants Generally. A defendant charged with the commission of a felony, who wishes to plead guilty, is required to plead personally. The court may require the personal appearance of a defendant charged with a misdemeanor.

(2) Organizational Defendants. An organizational defendant need not be present if represented by counsel who is present.

(b) Entry of Plea. A person charged with a criminal offense in county or circuit court, who is represented by counsel, may appear before the court at any time the judge may fix, be arraigned, enter a plea of guilty to the offense charged or, with leave of the court in misdemeanor cases, *nolo contendere*, and be sentenced at that time or some future time set by the court.

(c) Voluntariness. Before the trial court may accept a plea of guilty, the court must determine that the plea is voluntarily and intelligently made and that there is a factual basis for the plea. A plea is not voluntary if induced by fear, violence, deception, or improper inducements. A showing that the plea of guilty was voluntarily and intelligently made must appear in the record.

(d) Advice to the Defendant. When the defendant is arraigned and wishes to plead guilty to a felony or a misdemeanor with the possibility of incarceration, the defendant may be placed under oath and it is the duty of the trial court to address the defendant personally in open court to inquire and determine:

> (1) That the accused is competent to understand the nature of the charge;

> (2) That the accused understands the nature and consequences of the plea, and the maximum and minimum penalties provided by law;

> (3) That the accused understands that, by pleading guilty, the accused waives the constitutional rights of trial by jury, the right to confront and cross-examine adverse witnesses, and the right against self-incrimination; as well as that, if the accused is not represented by an attorney, that the accused is aware of the right to an attorney at every stage of the proceeding and that one will be appointed to represent the accused, if indigent; and

(4) That the accused understands that, if the accused is not a citizen of the United States, the plea may have immigration consequences. The court shall specify that, if convicted, a defendant who is not a United States citizen may be removed from the United States, denied citizenship, and denied admission to the United States in the future.

Comment

Rule 15.3(a) and (b) are largely derived from former Rules 8.03 and 8.04 of the Uniform Rules of Circuit and County Court. They adopt the requirement that, in all felony cases, the court shall address an individual defendant personally, in open court, and in the presence of counsel (unless counsel has been waived pursuant to Rule 7.1(c)). *See McCarthy v. United States*, 394 U.S. 459, 465-66, 89 S. Ct. 1166, 1170, 22 L. Ed. 2d 418 (1969). The Rule allows an organizational defendant to plead guilty through counsel who is present in court, as in Federal Rule of Criminal Procedure 43(b)(1).

Section (c) comes directly from former Rule 8.04(A.)(3.) of the Uniform Rules of Circuit and County Court. Under section (c), the court must determine that the plea is made voluntarily with understanding of the nature of the charge; that is, that the defendant understands "what the plea connotes and . . . its consequence[,]" as required by *Boykin v. Alabama*, 395 U.S. 238, 244, 89 S. Ct. 1709, 1712, 23 L. Ed. 2d 274 (1969). The court must also satisfy itself that there is a factual basis for the plea before entering judgment. The normal consequence of a determination that there is not a factual basis for the plea would be for the court to set aside the plea and enter a plea of not guilty. The record should affirmatively reflect the questions asked and the defendant's responses, thereby providing an adequate basis for review.

Section (d) is largely derived from former Rule 8.04(A.)(4.) of the Uniform Rules of Circuit and County Court. The Rule extends to pleas involving misdemeanors with the possibility of incarceration. *See, e.g.,* Miss. Code Ann. §§ 63-11-30(2)(a) (first offense DUI), 97-3-7(1)(a) (simple assault). Section (d) prescribes the advice that the court must give to the defendant as a prerequisite to the acceptance of a guilty plea and requires the court to determine that the defendant understands the sentencing implications of that plea. Section (d) also identifies the constitutional rights that the defendant waives by the plea, which is designed to satisfy the requirements of understanding waiver set forth in **Boykin**.

Generally speaking, it is within the court's discretion as to whether and to what extent to advise the defendant of "collateral consequences" of a plea of guilty or *nolo contendere*. *See* **Magyar v. State**, 18 So. 3d 807, 811-12 (Miss. 2009) ("there is no requirement that a defendant be informed of the collateral consequences" of a guilty plea; duty to register as a sex offender deemed a "collateral consequence" of a guilty plea). But immigration consequences stand as an exception; under Rule 15.3(d)(4), disclosure of certain potential immigration consequences is mandatory. *See* **Padilla v. Kentucky**, 559 U.S. 356, 130 S. Ct. 1473, 176 L. Ed. 2d 284 (2010) (deficient performance under the ineffective assistance of counsel standard in **Strickland v. Washington**, 466 U.S. 668, 104 S. Ct. 2052, 80 L. Ed. 2d 674 (1984), when counsel failed to advise defendant that his guilty plea made him subject to automatic deportation); Fed. R. Crim. P. 11(b)(1)(O).

Rule 15.4 Plea Bargaining.
(a) Entering into Plea Agreements.
(1) The prosecuting attorney is encouraged to discuss and agree on pleas which may be entered by the defendant. Any discussions or agreements must be conducted with defendant's attorney or, if defendant is unrepresented, the discussion and agreement may be conducted with the defendant.

(2) The prosecuting attorney and the defendant's attorney, or the defendant acting *pro se*, may reach an agreement that upon entry of a plea of guilty or, with leave of the court in misdemeanor cases, *nolo contendere*, to the offense charged or to a lesser or related offense, the prosecuting attorney may do any of the following:

(A) Move for a dismissal of other charges;

(B) Make a recommendation to the trial court for a particular sentence, with the understanding that such recommendation or request will not be binding upon the court; or

(C) Make a recommendation to the trial court for a particular sentence, which the court may accept or reject. If the court accepts the plea agreement, it must inform the defendant the agreed disposition will be included in the judgment. If the court rejects the recommendation, the court must do the following on the record:

> (i) inform the parties that the court rejects the plea agreement;

> (ii) advise the defendant personally that the court is not required to follow the plea agreement and give the defendant an opportunity to withdraw the plea; and

> (iii) advise the defendant personally that if the plea is not withdrawn, the court may dispose of the case less favorably toward the defendant than the plea agreement contemplated.

(3) Defense attorneys shall not conclude any plea bargaining on behalf of the defendant without the defendant's full and complete consent, being certain that the decision to plead is made by defendant. Defense attorneys must advise the defendant of all pertinent matters bearing on the choice of plea, including likely results or alternatives.

(b) Disclosure and Consideration of Plea Agreement. The trial judge shall not participate in any plea discussion. The court may designate a cut-off date for plea discussions and may refuse to consider the recommendation after that date. After a recommended disposition on the plea has been reached, it may be made known to the court, along with the reasons for the recommendation, prior to the acceptance of the plea. The court shall require disclosure of the recommendation in open court, with the terms of the recommendation to be placed in the record.

(c) Withdrawing a Plea.
(1) It is within the discretion of the court to permit or deny a motion for the withdrawal of a guilty plea, except as provided in (a)(2).

(2) In order to be sufficient, a motion to withdraw a guilty plea must show good cause.

(d) Inadmissibility of Withdrawn Guilty Plea. The fact that the defendant may have entered a plea of guilty to the offense charged may not be used against the defendant at trial if the plea has been withdrawn.

Comment

Rule 15.4(a) and (b) are largely derived from former Rule 8.04(B.) of the Uniform Rules of Circuit and County Court. Under Mississippi law, "a trial court is not bound to accept a defendant's guilty plea or enforce a plea agreement reached between the prosecutor and defendant." *Wilson v. State*, 21 So. 3d 572, 578 (Miss. 2009) (quoting *Wade v. State*, 802 So. 2d 1023, 1028 (Miss. 2001)). "Related" offenses under Rule 15.4(a)(2) means those offenses that could be joined in the same indictment under Rule 14.2(a).

Rule 15.4(c) and (d) are taken from former Rule 8.04(A.)(5.) - (7.) of the Uniform Rules of Circuit and County Court.

Rule 15.4(c) only applies in cases in which a defendant is to plead guilty or, with leave of the court in misdemeanor cases, *nolo contendere*, pursuant to a plea agreement. The Rule does not apply when a court imposes conditions pursuant to an offered, but unaccepted or nonadjudicated, plea under Mississippi Code Section 99-15-26. *See Brown v. State*, 533 So. 2d 1118 (Miss. 1988) (trial court not required to allow defendant to withdraw his guilty plea and enter plea of not guilty after he violated court-imposed conditions).

During the course of plea negotiations, a defendant enjoys the right to effective assistance of counsel. *See Missouri v. Frye*, 132 S. Ct. 1399, 182 L. Ed. 2d 379 (2012) (counsel's performance deemed deficient as defendant entered an open plea of guilty after a more favorable plea offer expired without being communicated by defense counsel); *Lafler v. Cooper*, 132 S. Ct. 1376, 182 L. Ed. 2d 398 (2012) (defense counsel rendered deficient performance in advising defendant to reject favorable plea offer and go to trial); *Burrough v. State*, 9 So. 3d 368, 375 (Miss. 2009). In *Frye*, the United States Supreme Court suggested that:

> [t]he prosecution and the trial courts may adopt some measures to help ensure against late, frivolous, or fabricated claims after a later, less advantageous plea offer has been accepted or after a trial leading to conviction with resulting harsh consequences. First, the fact of a formal offer means that its terms and its processing can be documented so that what took place in the negotiation process becomes more clear if some later inquiry turns on the conduct of earlier pretrial negotiations. Second, States may elect to follow rules that all offers must be in writing, again to ensure against later misunderstandings or fabricated charges. Third, formal offers can be made part of the record at any subsequent plea proceeding or before a trial on the merits, all to ensure that a defendant has been fully advised before those further proceedings commence.

Frye, 132 S. Ct. at 1409 (internal citations omitted).

Rule 16. Pretrial Motions

Rule 16.1 Motion Deadline; Hearings and Rulings on Motions.
(a) Motion Deadline. At arraignment or thereafter, the court may set a reasonable deadline for the filing and hearing of all pretrial motions. Pretrial motions shall include, but are not limited to, motions: to dismiss, to suppress evidence, to request discovery, for continuance, for severance, for appointment

of experts, for mental examination, or for any other matters which may delay the trial.

(b) Ruling on a Motion Generally. The court must decide every pretrial motion before trial unless it finds good cause to defer a ruling. When factual issues are involved in deciding a motion, the court must state its essential findings on the record.

Comment
Rule 16.1 tracks former Rule 8.02 of the Uniform Rules of Circuit and County Court. The Rule encourages the making of motions prior to trial, whenever possible, and resolution in a single hearing rather than in a series of hearings.

Rule 16.2 Effects of Rulings.
(a) Effect of Granting Motion Based on Defective Charge. If the court grants a motion to dismiss based on a defect in instituting the prosecution or in the charge, the court may:

(1) order the defendant released; or

(2) upon motion of the prosecuting attorney and upon a finding by the court of probable cause, order the defendant's continued detention; or

(3) if the defendant is free on bail or recognizance, order the continuation of such bail or recognizance for a reasonable time to afford the prosecutor an opportunity to file a new charging affidavit.

(b) Motion to Suppress. If a motion to suppress is granted, any suppressed property that was seized shall be restored to its rightful owner, unless otherwise subject to lawful detention. However, no firearm shall be returned to a convicted felon.

(c) Statutes of Limitations Tolled. The running of the time prescribed by an applicable statute of limitations shall be tolled by the issuance of the indictment until such time as the court grants a motion to dismiss based on a defect in the commencement of the proceedings or in the charge, unless the court, in granting the motion, finds that the state has not made a good faith effort to proceed properly and that the defendant has been prejudiced by any resulting delay.

Comment

Rule 16.2(c) exists to avoid penalizing the state for an inadvertent technical error which has not prejudiced the defendant. Thus, if a motion to dismiss is granted due to a defect in the charge or in the institution of the prosecution, the time period for which the charging instrument was in effect is also tolled. Of course, section (c) is just one aspect of the law governing the running and tolling of a statute of limitations. *See* Miss. Code Ann. §§ 99-1-5 to -9.

Rule 17 Disclosure and Discovery

Rule 17.1 Scope.

Rules 17.2 and 17.3 apply in felony cases and in trials of misdemeanor cases in circuit and county court. Rule 17.10 applies in municipal and justice court. The balance of Rule 17 applies in all courts.

Comment

Rules 17.2 through 17.9 address discovery in the context of felony cases and trials of misdemeanor cases in circuit and county court. Rule 17.10 expands current practice and creates a limited discovery procedure in municipal and justice courts.

Rule 17.2 Disclosure by the Prosecution.

Subject to the exceptions of Rule 17.6(a) and 17.7, the prosecution must disclose to each defendant or to the defendant's attorney, and permit the defendant or defendant's attorney to inspect, copy, test, and photograph upon written request and without the necessity of court order, the following which is in the possession, custody, or control of the State, the existence of which is known or by the exercise of due diligence may become known to the prosecution:

(1) Names and addresses of all witnesses in chief proposed to be offered by the prosecution at trial, together with a copy of the contents of any statement (written, recorded or otherwise preserved) of each such witness and the substance of any oral statement made by any such witness;

(2) Copy of any written or recorded statement of the defendant and the substance of any oral statement made by the defendant;

(3) Copy of the criminal record of the defendant;

(4) Any reports, statements, or opinions of experts (written, recorded or otherwise preserved) made in connection with the particular case and the substance of any oral statement made by any such expert;

(5) Any physical evidence, photographs, and data or information that exists in electronic or magnetic form relevant to the case or which may be offered in evidence; and

(6) Any exculpatory material concerning the defendant.

Upon a showing of materiality to the preparation of the defense, the court may mandate such other discovery to the defendant's attorney as justice may require.

Comment

Rule 17.2 is derived from former Rule 9.04(A.) of the Uniform Rules of Circuit and County Court.

Rule 17.3 Disclosure by Defendant.

If the defendant requests discovery under Rule 17, the defendant shall, subject to constitutional limitations, promptly disclose to the prosecutor and permit the prosecutor to inspect, copy, test, and photograph the following information and material which corresponds to that which the defendant sought and which is in the possession, custody, or control of the defendant or the defendant's attorney, or the existence of which is known, or by the exercise of due diligence may become known, to the defendant or defendant's counsel:

(1) Names and addresses of all witnesses in chief which the defendant may offer at trial, together with a copy of the contents of any statement (written, recorded or otherwise preserved) of each such witness and the substance of any oral statement made by any such witness;

(2) Any physical evidence, photographs, and data or information that exists in electronic or magnetic form which the defendant may offer in evidence; and

(3) Any reports, statements, or opinions of experts which the defendant may offer in evidence.

Comment

Rule 17.3 tracks former Rule 9.04(C.) of the Uniform Rules of Circuit and County Court.

Rule 17.4 Notice of Defenses.
(a) Alibi Defense.
(1) In General. Upon the written demand of the prosecuting attorney stating the time, date, and place at which the alleged offense was committed, the defendant shall serve within ten (10) days, or at such other time as the court may direct, upon the prosecuting attorney, a written notice of the intention to offer a defense of alibi, which notice shall state the specific place(s) at which the defendant claims to have been at the time of the alleged offense and the names and addresses of the witnesses upon whom the defendant intends to rely to establish such alibi.

Within ten (10) days thereafter, but in no event less than ten (10) days before the trial, unless the court otherwise directs, the prosecuting attorney shall serve upon the defendant or the defendant's attorney a written notice stating the names and addresses of the witnesses upon whom the State intends to rely to establish the defendant's presence at the scene of the alleged offense and any other witnesses to be relied on to rebut testimony of any of the defendant's alibi witnesses.

If, prior to or during trial, a party learns of an additional witness whose identity, if known, should have been included in the information previously furnished, the party shall promptly notify the other party or the other party's attorney of the name and address of such additional witness.

(2) Effect of Failure to Comply. Upon the failure of either party to comply with subsection (a)(1), the court may use such sanctions as it deems proper, including:

(A) Granting a continuance;

(B) Limiting further discovery of the party failing to comply;

(C) Finding the attorney failing to comply in contempt; or

(D) Excluding the testimony of the undisclosed witness.

(3) Additional Provisions. Subsections (a)(1) and (a)(2) do not limit the defendant's right to testify in the defendant's own behalf.

(b) Insanity Defense.
(1) In General. If a defendant intends to rely upon the defense of insanity at the time of the alleged crime, the defendant shall, within the time provided for filing pretrial motions or at such later time as the court may direct, serve upon the prosecuting attorney and the clerk of the court a written notice of the intention to offer a defense of insanity.

Within ten (10) days thereafter, but in no event less than ten (10) days before the trial, unless the court otherwise directs, the defendant shall serve upon the prosecuting attorney the names and addresses of the witnesses upon whom the defendant intends to rely to establish the defense of insanity.

If a defendant intends to introduce expert testimony relating to a mental illness, defect, or other condition bearing upon the issue of whether the defendant had the mental state required for the offense charged, the defendant shall, within the time provided for the filing of pretrial motions or at such later time as the court may direct, serve upon the prosecuting attorney and the clerk of the court notice of such intention, with the names and addresses of such expert witnesses upon whom the defendant intends to rely.

The prosecuting attorney shall serve notice on the defendant promptly, but in no event less than ten (10) days prior to trial, stating the names and addresses of any witnesses upon whom the State intends to rely relating to the issue of the defendant's mental condition at the time of the alleged offense or the defendant's mental state required for the offense charged.

If, prior to or during trial, either party learns of an additional witness whose identity should have been included in the notice under this rule, the party shall promptly notify the other party or the other party's attorney of the name and address of such additional witness.

(2) Effect of Failure to Comply. If there is a failure to comply with the requirements of subsection (b)(1), the court may use such sanctions as it deems proper, including:

    (A) Granting a continuance and/or assessing costs against the appropriate attorney or party;

    (B) Limiting further discovery of the party failing to comply;

    (C) Finding the attorney failing to comply in contempt; or

(D) Excluding the testimony of appropriate witnesses.

(c) Exceptions. For good cause shown, the court may grant an exception to the requirements of sections (a) and (b).

Comment

Rule 17.4, based upon former Rules 9.05 and 9.07 of the Uniform Rules of Circuit and County Court, addresses the defendant's duty to provide written notice to the prosecuting attorney of any intention to introduce evidence at trial raising the defenses of alibi and/or insanity.

Rule 17.5 Depositions.
(a) When Taken.
(1) In General. A party may move that a prospective witness be deposed in order to preserve testimony for trial. The court may grant the motion because of exceptional circumstances and in the interest of justice. If the court orders the deposition to be taken, it may also require the deponent to produce at the deposition any designated material that is not privileged, including any book, paper, document, record, recording, or data.

(2) Detained Material Witness. A witness who is detained under Mississippi Code Section 99-15-7 may request to be deposed by filing a written motion and giving notice to the parties. The court may then order that the deposition be taken and may discharge the witness after the witness has signed under oath the deposition transcript.

(b) Notice.
(1) In General. A party seeking to take a deposition must give every other party reasonable written notice of the deposition's date and location. The notice must state the name and address of each deponent. If requested by a party receiving the notice, the court may, for good cause, change the deposition's date or location.

(2) To the Custodial Officer. A party seeking to take the deposition must also notify the officer who has custody of the defendant of the scheduled date and location.

(c) Defendant's Presence.
(1) Defendant in Custody. The officer who has custody of the defendant must produce the defendant at the deposition and keep the defendant in the witness's presence during the examination, unless the defendant:

> (A) waives in writing the right to be present; or

> (B) persists in disruptive conduct justifying exclusion after being warned by the court that disruptive conduct will result in the defendant's exclusion.

(2) Defendant Not in Custody. A defendant who is not in custody has the right, upon request, to be present at the deposition, subject to any conditions imposed by the court. If the State tenders the defendant's expenses as provided in section (d), but the defendant still fails to appear, the defendant – absent good cause – waives both the right to appear and any objection to the taking and use of the deposition based on that right.

(d) Expenses. If the deposition was requested by the State, the court may – or, if the defendant is unable to bear the deposition expenses, must – order the State to pay:

> (1) any reasonable travel and subsistence expenses of the defendant and the defendant's attorney to attend the deposition; and

> (2) the costs of the deposition transcript.

(e) Manner of Taking. Unless these Rules or a court order provides otherwise, a deposition must be taken and filed in the same manner as a deposition in a civil action, except that:

(1) A defendant may not be deposed without that defendant's consent.

(2) The scope and manner of the deposition examination and cross-examination must be the same as would be allowed during trial.

(3) The State must provide to the defendant or the defendant's attorney, for use at the deposition, any statement of the deponent in the State's possession to which the defendant would be entitled at trial.

(4) The trial judge may preside over the taking of the deposition.

(f) Use as Evidence. Depositions may be used in the manner provided by Mississippi Rule of Civil Procedure 32.

(g) Objections. A party objecting to deposition testimony or evidence must state the grounds for the objection during the deposition.

(h) Depositions by Agreement Permitted. The parties may, by agreement, take and use a deposition with the court's consent.

Comment

Rule 17.5 is based upon Federal Rule of Criminal Procedure 15. As with federal practice, taking a deposition requires a court order and a showing of "exceptional circumstances." Depositions may be ordered by the court to preserve testimony or to take the statement of a witness in order that the witness may be released from incarceration. *See* Miss. Code Ann. § 99-15-7 (detention of material witness).

Section (c) gives the defendant a right to be present, as the purpose of the deposition is perpetuation of testimony for use at trial. A deposition cannot be used at trial without the defendant's consent if the defendant was not present at its taking and did not waive the right to be present in writing. *See **Pointer v. Texas***, 380 U.S. 400, 85 S. Ct. 1065, 13 L. Ed. 2d 923 (1965).

If deposition testimony is used at trial, the rights of the defendant under the Confrontation Clauses of Federal and State Constitutions must be respected. *See **Conners v. State***, 92 So. 3d 676 (Miss. 2012); ***Davis v. Washington***, 547 U.S. 813, 126 S. Ct. 2266, 165 L. Ed. 2d 224 (2006); ***Crawford v. Washington***, 541 U.S. 36, 124 S. Ct. 1354, 158 L. Ed. 2d 177 (2004).

Rule 17.6 General Standards.
In all disclosures under this Rule the following shall apply:

(a) Materials Not Subject to Disclosure.
(1) Work Product. Disclosure shall not be required of legal research or of records, correspondence, reports, or memoranda to the extent that they contain the opinions, theories, or conclusions of the prosecuting or defense attorney or members of legal staff.

(2) Informants. Disclosure of an informant's identity shall not be required unless the confidential informant is to be produced at a hearing or trial, a failure to disclose his/her identity will infringe the constitutional rights of the accused, and/or the informant was, or depicts himself/herself as, an eyewitness to the event(s) constituting the charge against the defendant.

(b) Use of Discovery Material. The attorney receiving discovery material is responsible for those materials and shall not distribute them to third parties.

(c) Advice from Counsel Regarding Relevant Information. Except as otherwise provided by law, or in cases where the witness would be forced to reveal self-incriminating evidence, neither an attorney for the parties nor other prosecution or defense personnel shall:

> (1) advise persons having relevant information or material, except the accused, to refrain from discussing the case with, or showing any relevant material to, the opposing attorney(s), or

> (2) otherwise impede the opposing attorney(s') investigation of the case.

(d) Filing Discovery Material. Discovery material shall not be filed with the clerk unless authorized by the court.

Comment

Rule 17.6 follows portions of former Rule 9.04(B.), (D.), (F.), and (I.) of the Uniform Rules of Circuit and County Court.

Rule 17.7 Excision and Protective Orders.
(a) Discretion of the Court to Deny, Restrict, or Defer Disclosure. Upon a showing of cause, the court may order that specified disclosures be denied, restricted, or deferred, or make such other order as is appropriate. For instance, the court may limit or deny disclosure if it finds that there is a substantial risk to any person of physical harm, intimidation, bribery, economic reprisals, or unnecessary annoyance or embarrassment resulting from such disclosure which outweighs any usefulness of the disclosure. However, all material and information to which a party is entitled must be disclosed in time to permit the party's attorney to make beneficial use thereof.

(b) Discretion of the Court to Authorize Excision. When some parts of certain materials are discoverable under these Rules and other parts are not discoverable, as much of the material should be disclosed as is consistent with the Rules.

(c) Protective and Excision Order Proceedings. In the event there are matters arguably within the scope of a party's discovery request or an order for discovery, and the opposing party is of the opinion that the requesting party is not entitled to discovery of same, the opposing party shall, as soon as is reasonably practicable, file with the clerk of the court a written statement describing the nature of the information or the materials at issue as fully as is reasonably possible without disclosure of same and stating the grounds for objection to disclosure. Subject to the limitations otherwise provided in these Rules, determinations such as whether the matters requested in discovery are relevant to the case, exculpatory, possible instruments of impeachment, and the like may be made only by the party requesting or to receive the discovery.

Upon request of any person, the court may permit any showing of cause for denial or regulation of disclosures, or portion of such showing, to be made *in camera*. A record shall be made of such proceedings. If the court enters an order granting relief following a hearing *in camera*, the entire record of such hearing shall be sealed and preserved in the records of the court, to be made available to the appellate court in the event of an appeal.

(d) Preservation of Record. Material excised pursuant to judicial order shall be sealed and preserved in the records of the court, to be made available to the appellate court in the event of an appeal.

Comment

Rule 17.7 is derived from portions of former Rules 9.04(B.), (G.), and (H.) of the Uniform Rules of Circuit and County Court. Section (a) gives the court broad discretion to limit the discovery required by this Rule whenever it is shown a risk of harm resulting from a specific disclosure.

Rule 17.8 Continuing Duty to Disclose.

Both the State and the defendant have a duty timely to supplement discovery. If, subsequent to compliance with these Rules or orders pursuant thereto, a party discovers additional material or information which is subject to disclosure, that party shall promptly notify the other party or the other party's attorney of the existence of such additional material or information and, if the additional material or information is discovered during trial, the court shall also be notified.

Comment

Rule 17.8 is based upon former Rule 9.04(E.) of the Uniform Rules of Circuit and County Court.

Rule 17.9 Failure to Disclose; Sanctions.

(a) Failure to Make Disclosure - Pre-Trial. If, at any time prior to trial, it is brought to the attention of the court that a party has failed to comply with an applicable discovery rule or an order issued pursuant thereto, the court may order such party to permit the discovery of material and information not previously disclosed, grant a continuance, or enter such other order as it deems just under the circumstances.

(b) Failure to Make Disclosure - Trial. If, during the course of trial, the prosecution attempts to introduce evidence which has not been timely disclosed to the defense as required by these Rules and the defense objects to the introduction for that reason, the court shall:

(1) Grant the defense a reasonable opportunity to interview the newly discovered witness and/or examine the newly produced documents, photographs or other evidence.

(2) If, after such opportunity, the defense claims unfair surprise or undue prejudice and seeks a continuance or mistrial, the court shall, in the interest of justice and absent unusual circumstances, exclude the evidence, grant a continuance for a period of time reasonably necessary for the defense to meet the non-disclosed evidence, or grant a mistrial.

(3) The court shall not be required to grant either a continuance or mistrial for such a discovery violation if the prosecution withdraws its efforts to introduce such evidence.

The court shall follow the same procedure for violation of discovery by the defense.

(c) Sanctions. Willful violation by an attorney of an applicable discovery rule, or an order issued pursuant thereto, may subject the attorney to appropriate sanctions by the court.

Comment

Rule 17.9 is modeled after former Rule 9.04(I.) of the Uniform Rules of Circuit and County Court. That rule addressed "the procedure trial courts should follow when confronted with a discovery violation" in the manner set forth in *Box v. State*, 437 So. 2d 19, 22-26 (Miss. 1983) (Robertson, J., specially concurring). *Galloway v. State*, 122 So. 3d 614, 633 n.3 (Miss. 2013). *See also Fulks v. State*, 18 So. 3d 803 (Miss. 2009).

Rule 17.10 Discovery in Municipal and Justice Courts.
(a) Discovery by the Defense. Upon written request made prior to trial, the prosecuting attorney shall provide to the defense the following:

> (1) the names of all witnesses expected to testify for the prosecution;

> (2) a copy of any written statement of the defendant;

> (3) a copy of the criminal record of the defendant, if proposed for use as impeachment;

> (4) a copy of laboratory reports or reports of any tests made;

> (5) any physical evidence, photographs, and/or electronic data to be offered in evidence;

> (6) a copy of any exculpatory material concerning the defendant; and

> (7) any affidavit used to obtain a search warrant in the case.

The prosecutor has a continuing duty to supplement any disclosure previously furnished.

(b) Reciprocal Discovery. The prosecuting attorney is entitled to reciprocal discovery of items (a)(1) - (7).

Comment
Discovery in justice and municipal court, as provided in Rule 17.10, is new to Mississippi practice.

Rule 18 Trial by Jury; Waiver; Selection and Preparation of Petit Jury; Prohibited Disclosures.

Rule 18.1 Trial by Jury.
(a) Generally.
(1) Qualifications. Jurors shall have the qualifications as required by law.

(2) Number of Jurors - Felony Cases. In felony cases, conviction requires the unanimous consent of twelve (12) impartial jurors.

(3) Number of Jurors - Misdemeanor Cases. A six (6) person jury shall be used in all criminal misdemeanor actions tried in justice or county court (including, in county court, whether the case originated in such court or was appealed from a lower court). In such cases, the unanimous consent of six (6) impartial jurors is required for conviction. If the case is in justice court, a trial by jury may be demanded as provided by law, although there is no right to a jury trial in justice court if the potential sentence is less than six (6) months in jail. Trial by jury is not available in municipal court.

(4) Alternate Jurors. The court may direct the selection of a sufficient number of alternate jurors.

(b) Waiver. The defendant may waive the right to trial by jury with consent of the prosecution and the court. In a death penalty case, the defendant may also waive the right to have a jury determine the penalty if the prosecution and the court concur. Regarding any such waiver:

> (1) Before acceptance, the court shall address the defendant personally, advise the defendant of the right to a jury trial, and ascertain that the waiver is knowing, voluntary, and intelligent.

> (2) A waiver of jury trial or sentencing under this Rule shall be made in writing or in open court on the record.

(3) For good cause shown, the court may allow the defendant to withdraw the waiver of jury trial or sentencing.

Comment

Article 3, Section 31 of the Mississippi Constitution provides that "[t]he right of trial by jury shall remain inviolate . . . ." Miss. Const. art. 3, § 31. Petit jurors shall be summoned and impaneled as provided by law. *See* Miss. Code Ann. § 13-5-1, *et seq*. In felony cases, conviction requires the unanimous consent of twelve (12) impartial jurors. *See Markham v. State*, 209 Miss. 135, 46 So. 2d 88 (1950). Mississippi Code Section 13-5-1 sets forth the qualifications for competent jurors.

Section (a)(3) continues the practice of former Rule 10.01 of the Uniform Rules of Circuit and County Court, in permitting misdemeanor cases to be tried before a six (6) person jury. But "there shall be no jury trial" in justice court when the "potential of incarceration is less than six (6) months in jail . . . ." Miss. Code Ann. § 99-33-9. Also, consistent with former Rule 12.02(C.) of the Uniform Rules of Circuit and County Court, the constitutional right to trial by jury does not apply unless the maximum possible sentence exceeds six (6) months. *See Harkins v. State*, 735 So. 2d 317, 318 (Miss. 1999) (citing *Lewis v. United States*, 518 U.S. 322, 116 S. Ct. 2163, 135 L. Ed. 2d 590 (1996)); *Hinton v. State*, 222 So. 2d 690, 692 (Miss. 1969). Mississippi Code Section 21-23-7 does not provide for a jury trial in municipal court.

Section (b) follows common practice. *See* Fed. R. Crim. P. 23(a). Section (b)(3) provides that the court can allow a withdrawal of waiver for good cause shown. When considering the withdrawal of waiver, the court should consider the convenience of witnesses, parties, and potential jurors.

Rule 18.2 Jury Information.

Before the *voir dire* examination, each party shall be furnished with a list of the names and addresses of the prospective jurors present and qualified to serve. Each party shall also be furnished with each prospective juror's employment status, occupation, employer, residency status, education level, prior jury duty experience, and felony conviction status. Further information may be required by the court.

Comment

Rule 18.2 provides for basic biographical information to be furnished to the parties. *See* Miss. Code Ann. § 13-5-1 (jury questionnaires).

Rule 18.3 Challenges.

(a) Preliminary Challenge to the Jury Panel. Any party may challenge the panel for good cause shown. Challenges to the panel shall be in writing or on the record, specifying the facts on which the challenge is based. Absent a showing of good cause, all such challenges shall be made and decided before the commencement of *voir dire*.

(b) Challenges for Cause. When there is reasonable ground to believe that a juror cannot render a fair and impartial verdict, the court, on its own initiative or on motion of any party, shall excuse the juror from service in the case. A challenge for cause may be made at any time, but may be denied for failure of the party making it to exercise due diligence. Challenges for cause and rulings thereon shall be made out of the hearing of the jurors, but shall be of record.

(c) Peremptory Challenges.
(1) In General. Both parties shall be allowed the following number of peremptory challenges for the selection of jurors:

(A) *Selection of Regular Jurors:* Regarding regular jurors, the defendant and the prosecution shall each have peremptory challenges, as follows:

(i) In cases wherein the punishment may be death or life imprisonment, the defendant and the prosecution each shall have twelve (12) peremptory challenges for the selection of the regular twelve (12) jurors.

(ii) In felony cases not involving the possible sentence of death or life imprisonment, the defendant and the prosecution each shall have six (6) peremptory challenges for the selection of the twelve (12) regular jurors.

(iii) The defendant and the prosecution each shall have two (2) peremptory challenges in a trial with a six (6) person jury.

These challenges may not be used in the selection of alternate juror(s).

(B) *Selection of Alternate Jurors:* When the court has elected to impanel alternate juror(s), the defendant and the prosecution shall each have peremptory challenges, as follows:

(i) In death penalty cases, the peremptory challenges shall equal the number of alternate jurors the court has ordered to be selected.

(ii) In all other cases, the peremptory challenges shall be one (1) challenge for each two (2) alternate jurors, or part thereof, ordered by the court to be selected.

These challenges for alternate jurors may not be used in the selection of regular jurors.

(2) Joint Trial of Several Defendants. When two (2) or more defendants are jointly tried, two (2) additional challenges shall be allowed to the defense and to the prosecuting attorney for each additional defendant. When two (2) or more defendants are jointly tried and cannot agree on the allocation of the peremptory challenges, they shall be exercised in the manner prescribed by the court.

Comment
Under section (b), "a juror who may be removed on challenge for cause is one against whom a cause for challenge exists that would likely [affect the

juror's] competency or . . . impartiality at trial." ***Evans v. State***, 725 So. 2d 613, 653 (Miss.1997), *cert. denied*, 525 U.S. 1133 (1999) (quoting ***Billiot v. State***, 454 So. 2d 445, 457 (Miss. 1984)). Section (b) permits a challenge for cause to be made whenever the cause appears. The trial court may deny the challenge if not seasonably made, but there is no absolute time limitation imposed by rule.

Section (c)(1) is consistent with former Rule 10.01 of the Uniform Rules of Circuit and County Court. Section (c)(1)(A)(iii) continues the practice in justice court regarding the number of peremptory challenges allowed. *See former* Uniform Rules of Procedure for Justice Court 1.19 (allowing two (2) peremptory challenges for the regular jurors and one (1) peremptory challenge for the alternate juror). Section (c)(2) expands on prior practice by providing two (2) additional challenges to the defense collectively, and to the prosecuting attorney, for each co-defendant. Co-defendants who cannot agree on the allocation of peremptory challenges will exercise them as directed by the court.

Rule 18.4 Procedure for Selecting a Jury.
(a) Oath. The court shall give all members of the panel the following oath:

> You, and each of you, do solemnly swear (or affirm) that you will true answer give to all questions asked you by or under the direction of the court, touching your qualifications as Jurors. So help you God.

(b) Inquiry by the Court; Brief Opening Statements. The court shall initiate the examination of jurors by identifying the parties and their counsel, briefly outlining the nature of the case, and explaining the purposes of the examination. The court shall ask any questions which it thinks necessary relating to the prospective jurors' qualifications to serve in the case on trial. The parties may, before *voir dire* and with the court's consent, present brief opening statements to the entire jury panel. On its own motion, the court may require counsel to do so.

(c) *Voir dire* Examination. The court shall permit the parties to conduct the examination of the prospective jurors and may itself conduct its own examination. The court may impose reasonable limitations with respect to questions allowed during a party's examination of the prospective jurors, giving due regard to the purpose of such examination.

(d) Scope of Examination. The examination of prospective jurors shall be limited to inquiries directed to bases for challenge for cause and information to enable the parties to exercise intelligently their peremptory challenges.

(e) Exercise of Peremptory Challenges. Following examination of the jurors, the parties shall exercise their peremptory challenges, in the order in which the jurors have been seated, as follows:

(1) the court shall rule upon all challenges for cause before the parties are required to exercise peremptory challenges;

(2) next, the prosecuting attorney shall tender a full panel of accepted jurors to the defendant(s), after having exercised any peremptory challenges desired;

(3) next, the defendant(s) shall go down the juror list accepted by the prosecuting attorney and exercise any peremptory challenges to that panel;

(4) once the defendant(s) exercise peremptory challenges to the panel tendered, the prosecuting attorney shall then be required to tender sufficient additional jurors to constitute a full panel of accepted jurors;

(5) the above procedure shall be repeated until a full panel of jurors has been accepted by all parties; and

(6) once the jury panel is selected, alternate jurors shall be selected following the procedure set forth above for selecting the jury panel.

Constitutional challenges to the use of peremptory challenges shall be made at the time each panel is tendered. Peremptory challenges shall be made out of the hearing of the jurors, but shall be of record.

(f) Alternate Jurors. Alternate jurors, in the order in which they are called, shall replace jurors who, prior to the time the jury retires to consider its verdict, become unable or disqualified to perform their duties. An alternate juror who does not replace a regular juror shall be discharged at the time the jury retires to consider its verdict.

Comment

Under Rule 18.4(c), parties are entitled "to probe the prejudices of prospective jurors and investigate their thoughts on matters directly related to the issues to be tried." *Ross v. State*, 954 So. 2d 968, 989 (Miss. 2007). But under sections (c) and (d), the judge may reasonably limit the length and content of the parties' *voir dire*. The court should instruct counsel that *voir dire* is permitted to enable counsel to propound questions seeking relevant information from and about the jurors, but not to ask "hypothetical questions or attemp[t] to elicit a pledge to vote a certain way. . . ." *Id*. The court should be particularly sensitive to the prejudice which can arise from *voir dire* by an unrepresented defendant.

Section (e) continues the practice of former Rule 4.05 of the Uniform Rules of Circuit and County Court. It contemplates that all jury panel members will participate in *voir dire* examination by the judge and counsel. Following disposition of the for-cause challenges, the parties shall exercise their peremptory challenges, as specified. All issues under *Batson v. Kentucky*, 476 U.S. 79, 106 S. Ct. 1712, 90 L. Ed. 2d 69 (1986), must be raised each time a panel is tendered. Regarding constitutional challenges to the use of peremptory strikes, *see Johnson v. State*, 875 So. 2d 208 (Miss. 2004); *Berry v. State*, 802 So. 2d 1033 (Miss. 2001).

Section (f) is consistent with Mississippi Code Section 13-5-67. Whether to dismiss a juror for good cause and to replace that juror with an alternate is within the trial court's discretion; the decision will not be disturbed absent a showing of prejudice. *See **Vaughn v. State***, 712 So. 2d 721 (Miss. 1998). But alternates must be discharged when the jury retires to deliberate. *See **Folk v. State***, 576 So. 2d 1243 (Miss. 1991).

Rule 18.5 Oath and Preliminary Instructions.
(a) Oath of Jurors. The court shall, on the record of each trial, give the jurors the following oath or remind the jurors that they are still under the following oath:

> You, and each of you, do solemnly swear (or affirm) that you will well and truly try all issues and execute all writs of inquiry that may be submitted to you, or left to your decision by the court, or under its direction, during the present term, and true verdicts give according to the evidence. So help you God.

Additionally, in each capital case, the jurors shall be sworn to "well and truly try the issue between the state and the defendant, and a true verdict give according to the evidence and the law."

(b) Oath of Bailiffs. In capital cases, bailiffs may be specially sworn by the court, or under its direction, to attend on such jury and perform such duties as the court may prescribe for them.

(c) Preliminary Instructions. Immediately after the jury is sworn, the court, on the record, may instruct the jury concerning its duties, its conduct, the order of proceedings, and the elementary legal principles that will govern the proceeding.

Comment
Sections (a) and (b) are based upon Mississippi Code Sections 13-5-71 and 13-5-73.

Rule 18.6 Note Taking by Jurors.
(a) Note Taking Permitted in the Discretion of the Court. The court may permit jurors to take written notes concerning testimony and other evidence. If the court permits jurors to take written notes, jurors shall have access to their

notes during deliberations. Those notes shall be secured in the custody of the clerk when court is not in session. Immediately after the jury has rendered its verdict, all notes shall be collected by the bailiff or clerk and destroyed.

(b) Instructions. The court shall instruct the jury as to whether note taking will be permitted. If the court permits jurors to take written notes, the trial judge shall give both a preliminary instruction and an instruction at the close of all the evidence on the appropriate use of juror notes. These instructions shall be given in the following manner:

(1) Preliminary Instruction: Note Taking Forbidden.

You may not take notes during the course of the trial. There are several reasons for this. It is difficult to take notes and, at the same time, pay attention to what a witness is saying. Further, in a group the size of yours, certain persons will take better notes than others will, and there is a risk that jurors who do not take good notes will depend on jurors who do. The jury system depends upon all jurors paying close attention and arriving at a decision. I believe that the jury system works better when the jurors do not take notes.

You will notice that we do have an official court reporter making a record of the trial; however, we will not have typewritten transcripts of this record available for your use in reaching a decision in this case.

(2) Preliminary Instruction: Note Taking Permitted.

If you would like to do so, you may take notes during the course of the trial. On the other hand, you are not required to take notes if you prefer not to do so. Each of you should make your own decision about this. If you decide to take notes, be careful not to get so involved in note taking that you become distracted from the ongoing proceedings.

Notes are only a memory aid and a juror's notes may be used only as an aid to refresh that particular juror's memory and assist that juror in recalling the actual testimony. Each of you must rely on your own independent recollection of the proceedings. Whether you take notes or not, each of you must form and express your own opinion as to the facts of this case. An individual juror's notes may be used by that juror only and may not be shown to or shared with other jurors. Immediately after the jury has rendered its verdict, all notes shall be collected by the bailiff or clerk and destroyed.

You will notice that we do have an official court reporter making a record of the trial; however, we will not have typewritten transcripts of this record available for your use in reaching a decision in this case.

(3) Use of Notes During Deliberations.

Jury Instruction #

Members of the Jury, shortly after you were selected I informed you that you could take notes and I instructed you as to the appropriate use of any notes that you might take. Most importantly, an individual juror's notes may be used by that juror only and may not be shown to or shared with other jurors. Notes are only a memory aid and a juror's notes may be used only as an aid to refresh that particular juror's memory and assist that juror in recalling the actual testimony. Each of you must rely on your own independent recollection of the proceedings. Whether you took notes or not, each of you must form and express your own opinion as to the facts of this case. Be aware that during the course of your deliberations there might be the temptation to allow notes to cause certain portions of the evidence to receive undue emphasis and receive attention out of proportion to the entire evidence. But a juror's memory or impression is entitled to no greater weight just because he or she took notes, and you should not be influenced by the notes of other jurors.

Comment

Rule 18.6 is consistent with former Rule 3.14 of the Uniform Rules of Circuit and County Court. *See also* **Vardaman v. State**, 966 So. 2d 885, 893 (Miss. Ct. App. 2007).

Rule 18.7 Admonitions to Jurors.

In all cases, the court, among other matters it deems proper, shall admonish the jurors that they are not to:

(1) discuss among themselves any subject connected with the trial until the case is submitted to them for deliberation;

(2) converse with anyone else on any subject connected with the trial, until they are discharged as jurors in the case;

(3) permit themselves to be exposed to outside comments or news accounts of the proceedings, until they are discharged as jurors in the case;

(4) conduct independent research about the case, legal issues, and/or the parties involved;

(5) view the place where the offense was allegedly committed; or

(6) form or express any opinion on the case until it is submitted to them for deliberation.

The jurors shall report to the court any communications or attempts to communicate with them on the case or any subject connected with the trial. When the jury is reconvened, the court, in its discretion, may poll the jury to determine if the jury has complied with the court's instructions.

Comment

Rule 18.7 essentially incorporates former Rule 3.11 of the Uniform Rules of Circuit and County Court. The court is free to supplement the admonitions in any manner it deems proper. This Rule implicitly prohibits the use of cell phones and other electronic devices to engage in forbidden conduct.

Rule 18.8 Jury Sequestration.
(a) Death Penalty Cases. In a death penalty case, the jury shall be sequestered during the entire trial.

(b) Other Cases. In all other cases, the jury may be sequestered on request of either the defendant or the prosecuting attorney made at least forty-eight (48) hours in advance of the trial. The court may grant or refuse the request to sequester the jury. The court may, on its own initiative or upon request of either party, sequester a jury at any stage of a trial.

Comment

Rule 18.8 preserves practice under former Rule 10.02 of the Uniform Rules of Circuit and County Court. Sequestration is mandatory in death penalty cases, *see Simmons v. State*, 805 So. 2d 452 (Miss. 2001), and discretionary in other cases, *see Baldwin v. State*, 732 So. 2d 236 (Miss. 1999).

Rule 18.9 Prohibited Disclosures.
Prior to the conclusion of the trial, no defense attorney, prosecuting attorney, clerk, deputy clerk, law enforcement official or other officer of the court, may release or authorize release of any statement for dissemination by any means of public communication on any matter concerning:

(1) The prior criminal record of the defendant or the defendant's character or reputation;

(2) The existence or contents of any confession, admission or statement given by the defendant; or the refusal or failure of the defendant to make any statement;

(3) The defendant's performance on any examinations or tests, or the defendant's refusal or failure to submit to an examination or test;

(4) The identity, testimony, or credibility of prospective witnesses;

(5) The possibility of a plea of guilty to the offense charged, or a lesser offense; and

(6) The defendant's guilt or innocence, or other matters relating to the merits of the case, or the evidence in the case.

Comment

Rule 18.9 is based upon former Rule 9.01 of the Uniform Rules of Circuit and County Court.

Rule 19 Trial

Rule 19.1 Proceedings at Trial.
(a) Order of Proceedings. Following the impanelment of the jury, the trial shall proceed in the following order unless otherwise directed by the court:

(1) A summary of the charge and the plea of the defendant may be provided by the court. In summarizing the charge, all references to prior conviction(s) alleged as sentencing enhancers shall be omitted.

(2) The prosecuting attorney may make an opening statement to the jury, confining the statement to the facts the prosecutor expects to prove.

(3) The defendant (personally or by counsel) may make an opening statement to the jury at the conclusion of the State's opening statement or prior to the defendant's case-in-chief. The statement

shall be confined to a statement of the defense and the facts, if any, the defendant expects to prove in support thereof.

(4) The prosecuting attorney shall offer the evidence in support of the charge.

(5) The defendant (personally or by counsel) may then make an opening statement, if it was deferred, and offer evidence in defense.

(6) The prosecuting attorney shall then be allowed to offer evidence in rebuttal.

(7) The court may allow surrebuttal for good cause.

(8) The judge shall then read the instructions to the jury. The court clerk may read the instructions to the jury when the judge is unable by reason of physical infirmity.

(9) The prosecuting attorney may then make a closing argument to the jury. Thereafter, the defendant may make a closing argument to the jury. Failure of the prosecuting attorney to make a closing argument shall not deprive the defendant of the right to argue. The prosecuting attorney may then make a rebuttal argument, not to exceed one-half (½) of the prosecuting attorney's allotted time. If, after the prosecuting attorney's initial closing argument, a defendant declines to make a closing argument, the prosecuting attorney shall make no further argument.

(b) Enhancement of Punishment.
(1) Sentencing enhancements based upon prior conviction(s). In cases involving enhanced punishment based upon prior conviction(s), the trial shall proceed as follows:

(A) Separate trials shall be held on the principal charge and on the charge of previous conviction(s). In the trial on the principal charge, the previous conviction(s) will not be mentioned by the state or the court except as provided by the Mississippi Rules of Evidence.

(B) If the defendant is convicted or enters a plea of guilty on the principal charge then, unless there is an agreement or ruling to the contrary, a hearing before the court without a jury will be conducted on the previous conviction(s).

(2) Elevated crimes based upon facts required to be found by a jury.

(A) Other than the fact of a prior conviction, any fact that increases the penalty for a crime beyond the prescribed statutory maximum shall be submitted to a jury and must be proved beyond a reasonable doubt.

(B) When a prior conviction is an element of the principal charge, the fact of a prior conviction shall be submitted to a jury and proved beyond a reasonable doubt. However, the defendant may stipulate to, or waive proof regarding, the prior conviction and the trial court shall accept such a stipulation. The stipulation then shall be submitted to the jury with a proper limiting instruction.

Comment

Section (a) provides a presumptive method of proceeding at trial. Under section (a)(7), the court retains discretion to allow surrebuttal upon a showing of good cause. *See* **Moody v. State**, 841 So. 2d 1067, 1090 (Miss. 2003) (surrebuttal "is discretionary with the trial judge, who controls the manner and mode of examination of witnesses"). Pursuant to sections (a)(8) and (a)(9), the court will generally give final instructions to the jury before closing arguments of counsel in order to enhance jurors' ability to apply the applicable law to the facts; the court may wish, however, to withhold giving necessary procedural and housekeeping instructions until after closing arguments. *See* Rules 22(f), 23.1(a), and 23.3(a).

Section (b)(1) continues the practice under former Rule 11.03 of the Uniform Rules of Circuit and County Court in cases involving enhanced punishment based upon prior conviction(s). A jury resolves the principal charge, then the court determines whether the defendant satisfies the requirements for enhanced sentencing. *See, e.g.,* ***Nathan v. State***, 552 So. 2d 99, 106 (Miss. 1989); ***Seely v. State***, 451 So. 2d 213, 214-15 (Miss. 1984).

Section (b)(2)(A) is consistent with ***Apprendi v. New Jersey***, 530 U.S. 466, 120 S. Ct. 2348, 147 L. Ed. 2d 435 (2000), in that facts which increase the penalty beyond the statutory maximum, other than prior convictions, must be found by a jury. *See, e.g.,* Miss. Code Ann. § 41-29-142 (enhanced penalty based upon proximity to school, church, etc.); Miss. Code Ann. § 97-37-37(1) (general firearms enhancement); ***Taylor v. State***, 137 So. 3d 283, 287 (Miss. 2014) ("*Apprendi* requires the jury to find not the sentence enhancement itself, but every *fact* required for the sentence enhancement to be imposed") (emphasis in original); ***Brown v. State***, 995 So. 2d 698, 703 (Miss. 2008) ("The existence of a church within 1,500 feet of Brown's crime . . . is a fact that he was entitled to have determined by a jury").

Section (b)(2)(B) addresses instances in which a prior conviction is an element of the principal charge. *See, e.g.,* Miss. Code Ann. §§ 63-11-30(2)(c) (third and subsequent offense DUI), 97-37-5 (possession of firearm, etc., by a convicted felon), 97-37-37(2) (firearms enhancement applicable to "any convicted felon who uses or displays a firearm during the commission of any felony"). A criminal defendant is "indisputably entitle[d]" to "a jury determination that [he] is guilty of every element of the crime with which he is charged, beyond a reasonable doubt." ***Apprendi***, 530 U.S. at 477 (quoting ***United States v. Gaudin***, 515 U.S. 506, 510, 115 S. Ct. 2310, 132 L. Ed. 2d 444 (1995)). *See also* ***Smith v. State***, 950 So. 2d 1056, 1060 (Miss. Ct. App. 2007). Therefore, when a prior conviction is an element of the principal charge, that fact must be determined by a jury. *See* ***Sallie v. State***, 155 So. 3d 760, 762 (Miss. 2015) ("the jury must find the elements of the firearm enhancement beyond a reasonable doubt under *Apprendi* before a trial court may apply the enhancement"); ***Rogers v. State***, 130 So. 3d 544, 550 (Miss. Ct. App. 2013); ***Rigby v. State***, 826 So. 2d 694, 700 (Miss. 2002) ("This Court has repeatedly held that prior DUI convictions are necessary elements of a felony DUI charge. Thus, they must be proven beyond a reasonable doubt to the jury"). That said, the defendant may stipulate to the prior conviction(s), and such a stipulation "should be submitted to the jury with a proper limiting instruction." *Rigby*, 826 So. 2d at 702. In *Rigby*, the limiting instruction was addressed as follows:

> [t]he instruction should explain to the jury that the prior DUI convictions should be considered for the sole purpose of determining whether the defendant is guilty of felony DUI and that such evidence should not be considered in determining whether the defendant acted in conformity with such convictions in the presently charged offense.

Id. Additionally:

> [w]here evidence of a prior conviction is a necessary element of the crime for which the defendant is on trial (i.e., possession of firearm by a convicted felon), but evidence of the *specific nature of the crime* for which the defendant was previously convicted . . . , is not an essential element of the crime for which the defendant is on trial, as it is in DUI cases, the trial court should accept a defendant's offer to stipulate and grant a limiting instruction.

Williams v. State, 991 So. 2d 593, 605-06 (Miss. 2008) (emphasis in original). *See also* ***Herrington v. State***, 102 So. 3d 1241, 1248 (Miss. Ct. App. 2012) ("The jury did not need to know the details of Herrington's prior convictions to reach a verdict on the charge of felon in possession of a weapon; it needed only to know that there was one prior felony conviction. The type of prior conviction has no probative value regarding whether Herrington was a felon in possession of a weapon").

Rule 19.2 Bifurcated Trials.

(a) Death Penalty Cases. In any case in which the State seeks to impose the death penalty, the trial shall be conducted in accordance with Mississippi Code Sections 99-19-101 and 99-19-103, as amended, and applicable court decisions.

(b) Cases in Which the Jury May Impose Life Sentence.
(1) In all cases not involving the death penalty, in which the jury may impose a life sentence, the court may conduct a bifurcated trial. If the defendant is found guilty of an offense for which life imprisonment may be imposed, a sentencing trial shall be held before the same jury, if possible, or before the court if jury waiver is allowed by the court.

(2) At the sentencing hearing:

> (A) the prosecution may introduce evidence of aggravation of the offense of which the defendant has been adjudged guilty;

> (B) the defendant may introduce any evidence of extenuation or mitigation;

> (C) the prosecution may introduce evidence in rebuttal of the evidence of the defendant; and

> (D) a record shall be made of the above proceeding and shall be maintained in the office of the clerk of the trial court as a part of the record.

Comment

Rule 19.2 largely tracks the provisions in former Rules 10.04(A.) and (B.) of the Uniform Rules of Circuit and County Court. *See Taggart v. State*, 957 So. 2d 981, 991-95 (Miss. 2007) (discussing procedure in non-death penalty cases).

Rule 20 Duties of Court Reporters

(a) Felony Cases. In all felony cases, the court reporter shall make a record of the *voir dire* and selection of the jury, opening statements, bench and in-chambers conferences, and closing arguments, whether or not such is ordered by the judge or requested by either party. In death-penalty cases, this duty may not be abrogated by the judge or waived by the defendant, and is in addition to all other duties.

(b) Other Cases.
(1) Circuit and county court. In all other cases in circuit and county court, the court reporter shall make a record of the *voir dire* and selection of the jury, opening statements, bench and in-chambers conferences, and closing arguments, if directed to do so by the judge.

(2) Municipal and justice court. In criminal proceedings in municipal and justice court, either party may engage the services of a court reporter to take down the proceedings, at the expense of the requesting party.

Comment

Rule 20(a) places duties on court reporters which are in addition to all other duties imposed by law or the court. *See **Davis v. State**,* 684 So. 2d 643, 651 (Miss. 1996) (citation omitted) ("[t]he law obligates the court reporter to take notes of all proceedings at trial so that they will be available in the event of an appeal"). The duties of section (b)(1) apply only if the judge so orders. Section (b)(2) provides for either party to engage the services of a court reporter during criminal proceedings in municipal and justice court. While any such transcript will not constitute the official record, it may be used for other purposes (e.g., impeachment).

Rule 21 Motions for Directed Verdict
(a) After the Prosecution's Case-in-Chief. After the prosecution rests, the court, on its own motion or upon motion by the defendant, may consider whether the evidence is sufficient to sustain a conviction. A motion for directed verdict must specify the manner in which the evidence is deficient. When, with respect to one (1) or more elements of the offense charged, the evidence is insufficient to support a conviction, the court shall order a directed verdict of "not guilty." The trial shall proceed with respect to the remaining count(s), if any.

(b) At the Close of the Evidence. If the motion for directed verdict is denied, the defendant may rest or proceed to introduce evidence on his/her behalf. If the defendant chooses to go forward with his/her own case, the defendant may renew the motion for directed verdict after the close of all the evidence.

(c) Waiver. The failure of a defendant to challenge the sufficiency of the evidence at the times and in the manner prescribed will constitute a waiver of any argument on appeal pertaining to the sufficiency of the evidence to support the verdict.

(d) Denial by Operation of Law. If, for any reason, a motion or a renewed motion for directed verdict is not ruled upon by the entry of judgment, it is deemed denied for purposes of appellate review.

Comment

Rule 21 follows common-law practice for a motion for directed verdict. A motion for directed verdict goes to the sufficiency of the evidence. *See McClain v. State*, 625 So. 2d 774, 778 (Miss. 1993). All evidence introduced by the State, together with any reasonable inferences that may be drawn therefrom, is accepted as true. *See Davis v. State*, 530 So. 2d 694, 703 (Miss. 1988). The "critical inquiry" involves "whether the evidence shows 'beyond a reasonable doubt that [the] accused committed the act charged, and that he did so under such circumstances that every element of the offense existed; and where the evidence fails to meet this test it is insufficient to support a conviction.'" *Bush v. State*, 895 So. 2d 836, 843 (Miss. 2005) (quoting *Carr v. State*, 208 So. 2d 886, 889 (Miss. 1968)). To preserve the issue for appeal, the defendant must move for directed verdict at the close of the prosecution's case-in-chief. *See Page v. State*, 990 So. 2d 760, 762 (Miss. 2008). "If a motion for directed verdict is denied and the defendant introduces evidence on his own behalf, the defendant must renew his motion for directed verdict at the close of all evidence." *Id*. Failure to do so waives the issue on appeal. *See Seales v. State*, 90 So. 3d 37 (Miss. 2012).

Rule 22 Jury Instructions

(a) Procedural Instructions. At the commencement of and during the course of a trial, the court may orally give the jury cautionary and other instructions of law relating to trial procedure and the duty and function of the jury, and may acquaint the jury generally with the nature of the case. Every oral instruction shall be recorded by the court reporter as it is delivered to the jury. All other instructions shall be in writing.

(b) Substantive Instructions.
(1) By the Parties. At least twenty-four (24) hours before trial, or at such other time during the trial as the court directs, each party must file with the clerk and deliver to all counsel jury instructions on the forms of verdict and the substantive law of the case. Except for good cause shown, the court shall not entertain a request for instructions which have not been pre-filed. At the conclusion of testimony, each party may present to the judge up to six (6) pre-filed substantive instructions. The court, for good cause shown, may allow more than six (6) instructions to be presented.

(2) By the Court. The court's instructions, if any, must be in writing and must be submitted to the parties who, in accordance with section (d), must make their specific objections on the record. The court shall not comment upon the evidence.

(c) Identification.
(1) Caption. All instructions shall be captioned at the top of the page "Jury Instruction No. ___" in order to allow the court to number the instructions given in such sequence as it deems proper.

(2) Identifying Submitted Instructions. All instructions submitted shall be identified with letters and numerals placed in the bottom right corner of each page. The court's written instructions shall be numbered and prefixed with the letter *C*. The State's instructions shall be numbered and prefixed with the letter *S*. A defendant's instructions shall be numbered and prefixed with the letter *D*. In actions with multiple defendants, Roman numerals shall be used to identify the proposed instructions of each defendant; the Roman numerals shall be placed after the alphabetical designation *D*, and shall conform to the sequential listing of defendants as stated in the indictment. Instructions shall not otherwise be identified with a party.

(d) Objections. A party who objects to any portion of the instructions or to a failure to give a requested instruction must inform the court, on the record, of the specific objection and the grounds therefor before the instructions are presented to the jury. An opportunity must be given to object out of the jury's hearing.

(e) Rulings on Instructions. Prior to closing argument, the court shall rule on the requested instructions, marking each "given" or "refused," and all such instructions shall become part of the record.

(f) When Read. Instructions shall be read by the court to the jury before closing arguments. Instructions will not be given after closing arguments have begun, except when justice so requires. All given instructions shall be available to the parties for use during closing arguments, and will be carried into the jury room when the jury retires to consider its verdict.

Comment

Rule 22(a) - (c) largely follows the practice established by former Rule 3.07 of the Uniform Rules of Circuit and County Court and Rule 51 of the Mississippi Rules of Civil Procedure.

Section (d) reflects Mississippi practice and tracks Rule 30(d) of the Federal Rules of Criminal Procedure.

Section (f) requires the court to instruct the jury before closing arguments in order to give the parties an opportunity to argue to the jury in light of the exact language used by the court. Section (f) does permit the court, when justice so requires, to instruct the jury both before and after closing arguments, which assures that the court retains power to remedy omissions in pre-argument instructions or to add instructions necessitated by the arguments. In this regard, section (f) gives the court more latitude than former Rule 3.07 of the Uniform Rules of Circuit and County Court, which permitted post-argument instructions only to correct "extreme" cases of injustice.

Rule 23 Deliberations

Rule 23.1 Retirement of Jurors.
(a) Retirement. After closing arguments, the court may direct the jury to select one of its members as a foreperson to preside over the deliberations and to write and return any verdict. The court also may admonish the jurors that, until they are discharged as jurors in the cause, they may communicate upon subjects connected with the trial only while the jury is convened in the jury room for the purpose of reaching a verdict. The jurors shall then retire in the custody of the bailiff(s) and consider their verdict.

(b) Permitting the Jury to Disperse. Except in cases in which the jury has been sequestered, the court may permit the jurors to disperse after their deliberations have commenced, instructing them when to reassemble, and giving the admonitions of Rule 18.7.

Comment
Rule 23.1 is consistent with former Rule 3.10 of the Uniform Rules of Circuit and County Court. Jury sequestration is governed by Rule 18.8.

Rule 23.2 Materials Used During Deliberation.
Upon retiring for deliberation, the jurors shall take with them:

(a) forms of verdict approved by the court;

(b) a copy of the written instructions;

(c) their notes (if any); and

(d) such exhibits and equipment as the court shall direct.

Comment
Rule 23.2 incorporates portions of Rule 3.10 of the Uniform Rules of Circuit and County Court. Section (a) is broad enough to permit the court to provide either a separate "form of verdict" document, an instruction on the form

of the verdict, or both. Sections (a) through (c) are mandatory, and require that all verdict forms, written instructions, and any juror notes – as set out in Rule 18.6 – be taken to the jury room. Only section (d), regarding exhibits and equipment, is discretionary; discretion is vested in the court to determine whether to permit a jury to take back to the jury room exhibits which are, for example, contraband, dangerous, prone to destruction or theft, or excessively voluminous. *See Holloway v. State*, 809 So. 2d 598 (Miss. 2000); *Pettit v. State*, 569 So. 2d 678 (Miss. 1990).

Rule 23.3 Additional Instructions; Further Review of Evidence Prohibited.

(a) Additional Instructions. If the jury, after they retire for deliberation, desires to be informed of any point of law, the court shall instruct the jury to reduce its question to writing and the court, after affording the parties an opportunity to state their objections or assent, may grant additional written instructions in response to the jury's request.

(b) Further Review of Evidence Prohibited. After the jurors have retired to consider their verdict, the court shall not recall the jurors to hear additional evidence.

Comment

Rule 23.3 tracks former Rule 3.10 of the Uniform Rules of Circuit and County Court. The Rule covers the right of the jury to request (by way of a note to the judge) additional instructions after deliberations have begun. Additional instructions should not be given if the request concerns matters not in evidence or questions of law not pertinent to the case, or calls on the judge to express an opinion on a factual matter.

Rule 23.4 Assisting Jurors at Impasse.

If it appears to the court that the jury has reached an impasse in its deliberations, the court may, in the presence of counsel, make inquiry of the jury and require the jury to continue their deliberations, with an appropriate instruction.

Comment

Rule 23.4 is consistent with former Rule 3.10 of the Uniform Rules of Circuit and County Court. The Court has approved the following instruction to address the jurors' report of impasse:

> I know that it is possible for honest men and women to have honest different opinions about the facts of a case, but, if it is possible to reconcile your differences of opinion and decide this case, then you should do so.
>
> Accordingly, I remind you that the court originally instructed you that the verdict of the jury must represent the considered judgment of each juror. It is your duty as jurors to consult with one another and to deliberate in view of reaching agreement if you can do so without violence to your individual judgment. Each of you must decide the case for yourself, but only after an impartial consideration of the evidence with your fellow jurors. In the course of your deliberations, do not hesitate to reexamine your own views and change your opinion if you are convinced it is erroneous, but do not surrender your honest convictions as to the weight or effect of the evidence solely because of the opinion of your fellow jurors or for the mere purpose of returning a verdict. Please continue your deliberations.

Sharplin v. State, 330 So. 2d 591 (Miss. 1976) (rejecting the various forms of the so-called *Allen* charge, per *Allen v. United States*, 164 U.S. 492, 17 S. Ct. 154, 41 L. Ed. 528 (1896)).

Rule 23.5 Mistrials.

Upon motion of any party, the court may declare a mistrial if there occurs during the trial, either inside or outside the courtroom, misconduct by a party, a party's attorney(s), or someone acting at the behest of a party or a party's attorney(s), resulting in substantial and irreparable prejudice to the movant's case.

Upon motion of a party or its own motion, the court may declare a mistrial if:

(a) The trial cannot proceed in conformity with the law; or

(b) It appears there is no reasonable probability of the jury's agreement upon a verdict.

Comment
Rule 23.5 tracks former Rules 3.10 and 3.12 of the Uniform Rules of Circuit and County Court.

Rule 24 Verdict

Rule 24.1 Time and Form of Verdict.
When the jurors have agreed upon a verdict they shall be returned to the courtroom by the bailiff(s). The court shall ask the foreperson or the jury panel whether an agreement has been reached on a verdict. If the foreperson or the jury panel answers in the affirmative, the judge shall call upon the foreperson or any member of the panel to deliver the verdict, in writing, to the clerk or the court. The verdict of the jury shall be unanimous, but need not be signed. The court shall examine the verdict and, if found to be in proper order, the clerk or the court then shall read the verdict in open court in the presence of the jury. If neither party nor the court desires to poll the jury, or when a poll of the jury reveals the verdict is unanimous, and if the verdict is in the form required by Rule 24.3, the court shall order the verdict filed and entered of record. The court then shall discharge the jurors, unless a bifurcated hearing is necessary.

Comment
Rule 24.1 is based, in part, on former Rule 3.10 of the Uniform Rules of Circuit and County Court. *See also* **State v. Taylor**, 544 So. 2d 1387, 1389 (Miss. 1989). The provision that the verdict "need not be signed" is consistent with current practice. Polling the jury is governed by Rule 24.5.

Rule 24.2 Types of Verdict.
(a) General Verdicts. Except as otherwise specified by this Rule, the jury shall in all cases render a verdict finding the defendant either guilty or not guilty.

(b) Insanity or Intellectual Disability Verdicts. When the jury determines that a defendant is not guilty by reason of insanity or intellectual disability, the verdict shall so state.

(c) Different Counts or Offenses. If the jury is instructed on different counts, offenses, or degrees of offenses, the verdict shall specify each count, offense, or degree of offense of which the defendant has been found guilty or not guilty.

(d) Lesser-included Offense or Attempt. The jury may be instructed that it can return a verdict on any of the following:

(1) an offense necessarily included in the offense charged; or

(2) an attempt to commit the offense charged or an offense necessarily included therein, if such attempt is an offense.

Comment

Rule 24.2 specifies the type of verdicts the jury may return. Unless otherwise specified, general verdicts are required by Rule 24.2(a). The general verdict gives the jury discretion over the disposition of the case which it would not have if restricted to finding particular facts in special verdicts.

Section (b) provides for a verdict of not guilty by reason of insanity or intellectual disability, which are exceptions to the general verdict rule. *See* Miss. Code Ann. §§ 99-13-7, 99-13-9. An insanity verdict, which should include an additional jury determination of "whether the accused has since been restored to his sanity and whether he is dangerous to the community[,]" implicates the post-acquittal procedures outlined in Mississippi Code Section 99-13-7. Miss. Code Ann. § 99-13-7(1) (Rev. 2010). *See also* Miss. Code Ann. § 41-21-88 (2010).

Section (c) is consistent with former Rule 3.10 of the Uniform Rules of Circuit and County Court and requires the jury to specify the particular counts and degrees of the offense(s) of which it finds the defendant guilty or not guilty. These provisions ensure that the verdict will be clear and unambiguous.

Section (d) tracks Federal Rule of Criminal Procedure 31(c) and permits the jury to find the defendant guilty of any offense necessarily included in the offense charged, including an attempt to commit the offense, if such attempt is a crime. The rule places the responsibility for deciding what verdicts the jury may return on the court, restricting the jury to returning verdicts for which instructions have been given to it under Rule 24.3. Under Rule 14.1(e), the indictment gives notice to the defendant that the trial will concern all necessarily included offenses as well as the offense specified, without the need for an explicit statement to that effect. Rules 14.1(e) and 24.2(d) make clear that the prosecuting attorney, as well as the defendant, is entitled to an instruction on any offense set forth in section (d) for which there is evidentiary support and for which a verdict form is submitted to the jury.

Section (d) also substantively tracks former Rule 3.10 of the Uniform Rules of Circuit and County Court, with the exception that the current rule contains no provision for instruction on "lesser-related" offenses. Yet, pursuant to *Hye v. State*, 162 So. 3d 750 (Miss. 2015), "a criminal defendant no longer has the unilateral right under Mississippi law to insist upon an instruction for lesser-related offenses which are not necessarily included in the charged offense(s), i.e., so-called lesser-nonincluded-offense instructions." *Id*. at 751 (overruling *Griffin v. State*, 533 So. 2d 444 (Miss. 1988)). Therefore, (d) is consistent with existing Mississippi case law.

Rule 24.3 Necessity for Forms of Verdict.
Forms of verdicts shall be contained in the jury instructions for each offense charged and, where warranted by the evidence, the trial judge may instruct for any or all lesser-included or attempt offenses as provided in Rule 24.2(d). The defendant may not be found guilty of any offense for which no form of verdict has been submitted to the jury. If the verdict returned is not fully responsive, the court shall direct the jury to retire for further deliberations. The court may correct or complete the verdict, as to form only, in open court in the presence of the parties and the jury.

Comment

Rule 24.3 permits the jury to find the defendant guilty of the offense charged, an offense necessarily included in each offense charged, or an attempt to commit the offense charged or an offense necessarily included therein, if the attempt is an offense. The Rule places on the court the responsibility of deciding what verdicts the jury may return, restricting the jury to returning verdicts for which verdict forms have been submitted to it.

Rule 24.4 Partial Verdicts and Mistrial.
(a) Multiple Defendants. If there are multiple defendants, the jury shall return a verdict as to any defendant about whom it has agreed.

(b) Multiple Counts. If the jury cannot agree on all counts as to any defendant, the jury shall return a verdict on those counts on which it has agreed.

(c) Mistrial. If the jury cannot agree on a verdict on one (1) or more defendants or counts, the court may declare a mistrial as to those defendants or counts.

Comment
Rule 24.4 is based on Federal Rule of Criminal Procedure 31(b). The Rule provides that a jury may return partial verdicts, as to multiple defendants, multiple counts, or both. Former Rule 3.10 of the Uniform Rules of Circuit and County Court permitted partial verdicts in cases of multiple defendants.

Rule 24.5 Jury Poll.
After a verdict is returned, but before the jury is discharged, the court shall on a party's request, or may on its own, poll the jurors individually. If the poll reveals a lack of unanimity, the court may direct the jury to deliberate further or may declare a mistrial and discharge the jury.

Comment
Under Rule 24.5, a jury poll is mandatory on the request of either party. Its purpose is to determine with certainty that "each of the jurors approves of the verdict as returned; that no one has been coerced or induced to sign a verdict to which he does not fully assent." ***Humphries v. District of Columbia***, 174 U.S. 190, 194, 19 S. Ct. 637, 638-39, 43 L. Ed. 944 (1899). Failure to poll the jury

137

at the request of the defendant is reversible error. *See* ***McLarty v. State***, 842 So. 2d 590 (Miss. Ct. App. 2003); ***State v. Taylor***, 544 So. 2d 1387, 1389 (Miss. 1989). This Rule discourages post-trial efforts to challenge the verdict on allegations of coercion on the part of some of the jurors.

Rule 24.6 Miscellaneous Provisions.
(a) Defective Verdicts. If a verdict is so defective that the court cannot determine from it the intent of the jury, the court shall, with proper instructions, direct the jurors to reconsider the verdict. No verdict shall be accepted until it clearly reflects the intent of the jury. If the jury persists in rendering defective verdicts, the court shall declare a mistrial.

(b) Comments by the Court to Jurors. While it is appropriate for the court to thank jurors at the conclusion of a trial for their public service, such comments should not include praise or criticism of their verdict.

(c) Limits on Impeaching the Verdict. After the verdict has been received by the court and entered on the record, the testimony or affidavits of the jurors shall not be received to impeach the verdict, except as permitted by the Mississippi Rules of Evidence.

Comment
Rule 24.6 is taken directly from former Rule 3.10 of the Uniform Rules of Circuit and County Court.

Rule 25 Post-Trial Motions

Rule 25.1 Motion for a New Trial.
(a) Motion by Defendant. The court, on written motion of the defendant, may vacate any judgment and grant a new trial for the grounds set forth in section (b).

(b) Grounds. The court may grant a new trial for any of the following reasons:

(1) if required in the interests of justice;

(2) if the verdict is contrary to law or the weight of the evidence;

(3) if new and material evidence has recently been discovered which probably would produce a different result at a new trial and, by reasonable diligence, such evidence could not have been discovered sooner;

(4) if the jury has received any evidence, papers or documents, not authorized by the court, or the court has admitted illegal testimony, or excluded competent and legal testimony;

(5) if the jurors, after retiring to deliberate on the verdict, separated without leave of court;

(6) if the court has misdirected the jury in a material matter of law, or has failed to instruct the jury on all questions of law necessary for their guidance; or

(7) if, for any other reason, the defendant has not received a fair and impartial trial.

(c) Timeliness. A motion for a new trial shall be made within ten (10) days after entry of judgment (which, for purposes of this Rule, includes both adjudication of guilt and sentence). Upon good cause shown, the court may grant a reasonable extension thereof.

(d) Court's Own Motion. The court may, on its own motion and with the consent of the defendant and notice to the prosecuting attorney, order a new trial before the entry of judgment.

Comment

Rule 25.1 preserves practice under former Rule 10.05 of the Uniform Rules of Circuit and County Court, with a few modifications and additions.

Section (b)(7) modifies the former rule by explicitly adding that a new trial may be granted for any reason if the defendant has not received a fair and impartial trial. Section (c) clarifies that the time to make a motion for a new trial begins to run after entry of judgment, which includes adjudication of guilt and sentence. Under section (d), the court may order a new trial before the entry of judgment only with the consent of the defendant and notice to the prosecuting attorney. Problems of double jeopardy may arise when the court acts on its own motion without the consent of the defendant. *See United States v. Smith*, 331 U.S. 469, 67 S. Ct. 1330, 91 L. Ed. 1610 (1947). Under Rule 4(e) of the Mississippi Rules of Appellate Procedure, a defendant must file a notice of appeal within thirty (30) days after the date of the denial of any motion for a new trial or the date of imposition of sentence, whichever is later.

Rule 25.2   Motion to Vacate Judgment.
(a) Power of the Court. The court, on motion of a defendant or on its own motion, may vacate judgment and dismiss the case without prejudice if the indictment or charging affidavit did not charge an offense, or if the court was without jurisdiction.

(b) Timeliness. A motion to vacate judgment shall be filed within ten (10) days after entry of judgment. The court may act on its own motion in vacating judgment only during the period in which a motion to vacate judgment would be timely.

Comment

Rule 25.2 essentially continues practice under former Rule 10.05 of the Uniform Rules of Circuit and County Court. *See also Jefferson v. State*, 556 So. 2d 1016 (Miss. 1989).

The deadline established by section (b) tracks the deadline for a motion for a new trial under Rule 25.1. However, a motion to vacate judgment (unlike a motion for new trial) does not toll the time for filing a notice of appeal under Mississippi Rule of Appellate Procedure 4(e). Therefore, when a motion under Rule 25.2 has been filed but not decided at the time an appeal has been perfected, both trial and appellate courts will have jurisdiction of the case; if the trial court then grants the Rule 25.2 motion, the appeal may be mooted. *See* ***Gardner v. State***, 547 So. 2d 806 (Miss. 1989); ***Wilson v. State***, 461 So. 2d 728 (Miss. 1984).

Rule 25.3   Denial by Operation of Law.

A motion for a new trial or a motion to vacate judgment pending thirty (30) days after entry of judgment shall be deemed denied as of the thirtieth (30th) day after the motion was filed. However, the parties may agree in writing, or the court may order, that the motion be continued past the thirtieth (30th) day to a date certain within ninety (90) days after the motion was filed; any motion still pending after the date to which it is continued shall be deemed denied as of that date. The motion may be continued from time to time as provided in this Rule.

Comment

Rule 25.3 is new to Mississippi practice. The Rule promotes finality by providing that a motion for a new trial or a motion to vacate judgment shall not remain pending in the trial court for more than thirty (30) days after the motion was filed. This Rule thereby addresses the problem of when a timely post-trial motion is filed but is not decided or even noticed for a hearing. Such a case is then essentially in limbo, as the pending post-trial motion indefinitely postpones the running of the period for filing a notice of appeal and indefinitely delays finality in the case. This deadline may be extended by written agreement of the parties or court order to a date certain within ninety (90) days after the motion was filed. Multiple extensions of the deadline, which should be rare, are nonetheless permitted by Rule 25.3.

Rule 25.4   Clerical and Technical Errors.

After giving notice to the State and the defendant, the court may correct a clerical error in a judgment or order, correct an error in the record arising from oversight or omission, or correct a sentence that resulted from arithmetical, technical, or other clear error.

Comment

Rule 25.4 is similar to Mississippi Rule of Civil Procedure 60(a). It provides an efficient method for correcting clerical and technical errors appearing in judgments, orders, or other parts of the record. *See Shinn v. State*, 74 So. 3d 901 (Miss. Ct. App. 2011) (recognizing authority for correction of scrivener's or clerical error at any time). A motion to correct simple clerical mistakes may be made at any time.

Rule 26 Judgment

Rule 26.1 Definitions; Scope.
(a) Determination of Guilt. The term "determination of guilt" means a verdict of guilty by a jury, a finding of guilt by a court following a non-jury trial, or the acceptance by the court of a plea of guilty or *nolo contendere*.

(b) Judgment. The term "judgment" means the adjudication of the court based on the verdict of the jury, the plea of the defendant of guilty or *nolo contendere*, or on its own finding following a non-jury trial, that the defendant is guilty or not guilty. The term "judgment" may include both determination of guilt and sentence.

(c) Sentence. The term "sentence" means the pronouncement by the court of the penalty imposed upon the defendant after an adjudication of guilt.

(d) Scope. Rule 26 shall apply to death penalty cases only to the extent that a procedure is not otherwise provided.

Rule 26.2 Judgment; Time.
(a) On Acquittal. When a defendant is acquitted of any charge, judgment pertaining to that charge shall be pronounced and entered immediately.

(b) On Conviction.
(1) On a determination of guilt on any charge, judgment pertaining to that charge shall be pronounced and entered together with the sentence.

(2) On a determination of guilt, the court shall, after receipt of the presentence report (unless a presentence report is not required), set a date for sentencing.

(3) Sentence shall be imposed without unreasonable delay.

Comment

Rule 26.2 replaces portions of former Rule 11.01 of the Uniform Rules of Circuit and County Court.

When the defendant has been convicted, section (b) follows common practice of pronouncing judgment at sentencing. Because often there will be a period of delay between adjudication of guilt and determination of sentence, pronouncement of judgment of conviction and sentence will be delayed until sentencing has been completed. As under former Rule 11.01 of the Uniform Rules of Circuit and County Court, section (b)(3) requires the sentence be imposed "without unreasonable delay."

Rule 26.3 Presentence Report.

(a) In General. A presentence investigation may be conducted and a report thereof shall be made as required for cases where the court has discretion in imposition of sentence. Contents of this report shall be disclosed only to the parties. A copy of said report shall be delivered to both the prosecutor and the defendant or the defense attorney within a reasonable time prior to sentencing so as to afford a reasonable opportunity for verification of the material. Prior to the sentencing proceeding, each party is required to notify the opposing party and the court of any part of the presentence report which the party intends to controvert by the production of evidence.

(b) Content. The presentence report may contain, but is not limited to, the following information:

(1) a description of the offense and the circumstances surrounding it, not limited to aspects developed for the record as part of the determination of guilt;

(2) any prior criminal convictions of the defendant, or juvenile adjudications of delinquency;

(3) a statement considering the economic, physical, and psychological impact of the offense on the victim and the victim's immediate family;

(4) the defendant's financial condition;

(5) the defendant's educational background;

(6) a description of the defendant's employment background, including any military record and present employment status and capabilities;

(7) the social history of the defendant, including family relationships, marital status, residence history, and alcohol or drug use;

(8) information about environments to which the defendant might return or to which the defendant could be sent should probation be granted;

(9) information about special resources which might be available to assist the defendant, such as treatment centers, rehabilitative programs, or vocational training centers;

(10) a physical and mental examination of the defendant, if ordered by the court; and

(11) any other information required by the court.

(c) Excluded Content. The report shall not include:

(1) sources of information obtained on a promise of confidentiality; or

(2) information which would disrupt an existing police investigation.

(d) Special Duty of the Prosecuting Attorney. The prosecuting attorney shall disclose to the defendant any information within the prosecuting attorney's possession or control, not already disclosed, which would tend to reduce the punishment to be imposed.

Comment

Section (b) embraces former Rule 11.02 of the Uniform Rules of Circuit and County Court, with two (2) additions. Section (b)(3) now provides for a statement about the impact of the offense on the victim and the victim's immediate family. Section (b)(7) now provides for the report to include information about the defendant's alcohol or drug use.

Rule 26.4 Sentencing Hearing.
(a) Generally. If the court has either discretion as to the penalty to be imposed or power to suspend execution of the sentence, the court shall conduct a sentencing hearing in all felony cases, unless waived by the parties with consent of the court. The sentencing hearing may commence immediately after a determination of guilt or may be continued to a later date. If a presentence report is required, the sentencing hearing shall not be conducted until copies thereof have been furnished or made available to the court and the parties.

(b) Enhanced Punishment Based on Prior Conviction(s). Absent stipulation, the court shall hold a hearing in order to establish the alleged prior conviction(s) to determine the defendant's status as a habitual or enhanced offender. The prosecution must establish the defendant's prior conviction(s) beyond a reasonable doubt. If the defendant disputes any conviction presented by the prosecution, the court may allow the prosecution to present additional evidence of the disputed conviction.

(c) Evidence. Evidence may be presented by both the prosecuting attorney and the defendant as to any matter that the court deems probative on the issue of sentencing.

Comment

Under Rule 10.1, the defendant has the right to be present at the sentencing hearing under Rule 26.4 and at the pronouncement of sentence under Rule 26.5.

Under Rule 26.4(b), the court determines the defendant's status as a habitual or enhanced offender. Rule 26.4(b) does not contemplate those facts and elements necessary to enhance a sentence that are required to be found by a jury, which is addressed in Rule 19.1(b). *See also* ***Apprendi v. United States***, 530 U.S. 466, 120 S. Ct. 2348, 147 L. Ed. 2d 435 (2000).

Rule 26.5 Pronouncement of Judgment and Sentence.

(a) Pronouncement of Judgment. The judgment shall be pronounced in open court at any time after conviction, in the presence of the defendant (unless waived pursuant to Rule 10.1(b)), and recorded in the minutes of the court. If the defendant is found not guilty or for any other reason is entitled to be discharged, judgment shall be entered accordingly.

(b) Pronouncement of Sentence. In pronouncing sentence, the court shall:

(1) afford the defendant an opportunity, personally and/or through the defendant's attorney, to make a statement on the defendant's behalf before imposing sentence;

(2) state that a credit will be allowed on the sentence, as provided by law, for time during which the defendant has been incarcerated on the present offense; and

(3) explain to the defendant the terms of the sentence.

Comment

Section (a) continues provisions in former Rule 11.01 of the Uniform Rules of Circuit and County Court (sentence pronounced in open court in the presence of the defendant). Subsection (b)(1) preserves the defendant's right to be present at sentencing, also recognized by Rule 10.1, unless waived under Rule 10.1(b). Subsection (b)(2) requires the court, at the time of sentencing, to make sure the record accurately reflects the time already spent in custody. *See* Miss. Code Ann. § 99-19-23. The explanation of the sentence under subsection (b)(3) should include the terms of probation, the length and order of sentences if there are more than one (1), and whether the new sentence is to be served concurrently with, or consecutively to, a sentence that the defendant is then serving.

Rule 26.6 Fine, Restitution, and/or Court Costs following Adjudication of Guilt.

(a) Scope. Rule 26.6 applies only following a determination of guilt and, therefore has no applicability to pretrial diversion, non-adjudication, and the like.

(b) Method of Payment; Installments. When the defendant is sentenced to pay a fine, restitution, and/or court costs, the court may permit payment to be made within a specified period of time or in specified installments. Restitution shall be payable as promptly as possible, taking into account the defendant's indigency or economic ability to pay.

(c) Method of Payment; To Whom. Unless the court expressly directs otherwise:

> (1) the payment of a fine, restitution, and/or court costs shall be made to the clerk of court; and

> (2) monies received from the defendant shall be applied as follows:

>> (A) first, to pay any and all court costs (as designated by statute) assessed against the defendant;

>> (B) second, to pay any restitution the defendant has been ordered to make; and

(C) third, to pay any fines imposed against the defendant.

The clerk shall, as promptly as practicable, forward restitution payments to the victim.

(d) Court Action upon Failure of Defendant to Pay Fine, Restitution, and/or Court Costs. Upon the defendant's failure to pay a fine, restitution, and/or court costs, the court first must require the defendant to appear and show cause why said defendant should not be held in contempt of court. A summons requiring the defendant's appearance shall be personally served on the defendant and shall set forth the time and location of the hearing. If the defendant fails to appear, the court may issue a warrant for the defendant's arrest. During the hearing, the court shall inquire and cause an investigation to be made into the reasons for nonpayment, including whether nonpayment was willful or due to indigency or economic inability to pay. In that review:

(1) If it appears to the satisfaction of the court that nonpayment is not willful, the court shall enter an order allowing the defendant additional time for payment, reducing the amount thereof or of each installment, or revoking the fine or order of restitution or the unpaid portion thereof in whole or in part. However, the court shall not suspend or reduce an assessment imposed pursuant to Mississippi Code Section 99-19-73.

(2) If the court finds nonpayment is willful and finds the defendant in contempt of court, the court may direct that the defendant be incarcerated until the unpaid obligation is paid, subject, however, to section (e).

(e) Incarceration for Nonpayment of Fine, Restitution, and/or Court Costs. (1) Incarceration shall not automatically follow the nonpayment of a fine, restitution, and/or court costs. Incarceration may be employed only after the court has conducted a hearing and examined the reasons for nonpayment and finds, on the record, that the defendant could have made payment but refused to do so. In justice and municipal court, such finding shall be included in the court's order.

(2) After consideration of the defendant's situation, means, and conduct with regard to the nonpayment, the court shall determine the period of any incarceration, subject to the limitations set by statute.

(3) If, at the time the fine, restitution and/or court costs was ordered, a sentence of incarceration was also imposed, the aggregate of the period of incarceration imposed pursuant to this Rule and the term of the sentence originally imposed may not exceed the maximum term of imprisonment authorized for the offense.

Comment
Rule 26.6 replaces former Rule 11.04 of the Uniform Rules of Circuit and County Court.

Section (b) mirrors practice under Mississippi Code Section 99-19-20(1) and recognizes that not everyone assessed a fine or restitution will be able to make full payment on the day of assessment. In addition to allowing payment in installments, the court may require the defendant to work on public property; the rate earned will be applied to the payment. *See* Miss. Code § 99-19-20(1), (2)(c).

Section (c) provides that, unless the court expressly orders otherwise, payments shall be made to the clerk and allocated as provided in section (c)(2). "The term 'fine' means, in addition to the pecuniary punishment, all fees, costs, assessments and other charges required by law to be imposed in such cases." Miss. Code Ann. § 99-19-3. Court costs include those designated by statute. *See, e.g.,* Miss. Code Ann. §§ 25-7-13 (circuit court clerk fees), 25-7-25 (justice court fees), 25-7-27 (marshals and constables' fees). Fees owed to private collection and/or probation companies are not included in court costs. Section (c) also requires restitution payments be forwarded to the victim as promptly as practicable, as opposed to accumulating payments before remitting them to the victim.

Section (d) outlines the court's authority to inquire into and address non-payment or non-compliance, through contempt and other means, and provides reasonable alternatives to automatic incarceration. Section (d)(1) generally follows Mississippi Code Section 99-37-11, while section (d)(2) follows Mississippi Code Section 99-19-20(2). The court may address contempt by any other means provided by statute. *See, e.g.,* Miss. Code § 99-19-65 (clerk's issuance of execution of any portion remaining unpaid). Nothing in Rule 26.6 precludes, in an appropriate case, proceeding pursuant to Rule 27.

Section (e) governs incarceration for non-payment and limits incarceration to instances in which the defendant could have satisfied payment but refused to do so. A defendant should not be imprisoned automatically when alternative methods are available. *See **Bearden v. Georgia**,* 461 U.S. 660, 672, 103 S. Ct. 2064, 76 L. Ed. 2d 221 (1983); ***Tate v. Short***, 401 U.S. 395, 91 S. Ct. 668, 28 L. Ed. 2d 130 (1971) (denial of equal protection to limit punishment to payment of a fine for those who are able to pay, but to convert the fine to imprisonment for those who are unable to pay). Further, the period of incarceration, if any, is subject to Mississippi Code Sections 99-19-20 and 99-37-9. Section (e)(3) follows Mississippi Code Section 99-19-20(2)(b) and ***Williams v. Illinois***, 399 U.S. 235, 90 S. Ct. 2018, 26 L. Ed. 2d 586 (1970), which forbid imprisonment of an indigent defendant for non-payment beyond the maximum sentence authorized for the offense.

Rule 26.7 Consecutive or Concurrent Sentences.
Unless otherwise provided by law, the court may direct that the sentence being imposed will be served concurrently with, or consecutively to, any other sentence previously or simultaneously imposed upon the defendant by any court. When sentencing orders are silent, sentences shall run concurrently.

Comment
Rule 26.7 is based generally on Mississippi Code Section 99-19-21. The Rule is intended to encompass multiple charges arising from the same criminal episode, unrelated offenses for which sentence is imposed at one time, and a sentence imposed while the defendant is serving a sentence in Mississippi or elsewhere for another offense. Unless the sentencing order specifies otherwise,

sentences shall run concurrently. *See **Shinn v. State***, 74 So. 3d 901 (Miss. 2011) (citing ***Anderson v. State***, 288 So. 2d 852 (Miss. 1974)).

Rule 26.8 Entry of Judgment of Conviction and Sentence.
(a) Entry of Judgment and Sentence. The judgment is complete and valid upon its entry in the minutes.

(b) Entry of Order and Duty of Clerk. Immediately upon entry of an order or judgment of the court, the clerk of the court shall make a diligent effort to assure that all attorneys of record have received notice of the entry of the order or judgment.

Comment

Rule 26.8 applies only to a judgment of conviction; Rule 26.2(a) governs judgment of acquittal.

Pursuant to former Rule 11.01 of the Uniform Rules of Circuit and County Court, section (a) provides that a judgment of conviction and sentence are complete upon entry in the minutes. Rule 26.1(c) defines sentence as "pronouncement by the court of the penalty imposed" following "an adjudication of guilt." Rule 26.5 requires pronouncement of judgment and sentence both be made in open court, and Rule 26.2(b) provides that a judgment of conviction shall be "pronounced and entered together with the sentence . . . ."

Section (b) tracks former Rule 11.05 of the Uniform Rules of Circuit and County Court.

Rule 27 Probation

Rule 27.1 Initiation of Revocation Proceedings; Securing the Probationer's Presence.
(a) Initiation of Revocation Proceedings. If a probationer has violated a condition of probation or has acted contrary to a lawful instruction issued by the

supervising officer, the supervising officer or the prosecuting attorney may petition the sentencing court to revoke or modify probation.

(b) Securing the Probationer's Presence. Pursuant to a petition to revoke or modify, the sentencing court may, when appropriate, issue a warrant for the probationer's arrest or issue a summons directing the probationer to appear on a specified date for a revocation hearing.

(c) Arrest by Supervising Officer. The probationer may be arrested without a warrant by the supervising officer responsible for the probationer's supervision or by the officer's agent, pursuant to statute, for violation of a condition of probation imposed or an instruction issued.

Comment

Section (a) provides a mechanism for probation revocation that permits initiation of the proceeding by the supervising officer or the prosecuting attorney. The court may issue an arrest warrant or a summons to compel the probationer's appearance or, if necessary, the supervising officer (or the officer's agent) may take the probationer into custody without a warrant. *See* Miss. Code Ann. § 47-7-37(2).

Rule 27.2 Preliminary Hearing After Arrest.

Whenever a probationer is arrested for an alleged violation of probation, an informal preliminary hearing shall be conducted as prescribed by statute.

Comment

Rule 27.2 refers to the applicable statute(s) on preliminary hearings in the context of probation-revocation proceedings. *See, e.g.,* Miss. Code Ann. § 47-7-37(3). *See also* **Gagnon v. Scarpelli**, 411 U.S. 778, 786, 93 S. Ct. 1756, 1761, 36 L. Ed. 656 (1973) (citing **Morrissey v. Brewer**, 408 U.S. 471, 487, 92 S. Ct. 2593, 2603, 33 L. Ed. 2d 484 (1972)) ("[a]t the preliminary hearing, a probationer or parolee is entitled to notice of the alleged violations of probation or parole, an opportunity to appear and present evidence in his own behalf, a conditional right to confront adverse witnesses, an independent decisionmaker, and a written report of the hearing").

Rule 27.3 Revocation of Probation.
(a) Hearing. A hearing to determine whether probation should be revoked shall be held before the sentencing court, as prescribed by statute.

(b) Summary Disposition. The probationer may waive the hearing prescribed by Rule 27.3(a) and the sentencing court may make a final disposition of the issue, if:

> (1) the probationer has been given sufficient notice of the charges and sufficient notice of the evidence to be relied upon; and

> (2) the probationer admits, under the requirements of Rule 27.3(e), commission of the alleged violation.

(c) Presence. The probationer is entitled to be present at the hearing.

(d) Counsel.
(1) The probationer may be represented by retained counsel.

(2) Counsel shall be appointed to represent an indigent probationer if the probationer makes a colorable claim that:

> (A) the probationer has not committed the alleged violation of the conditions of probation or the instructions issued by the supervising officer; or

> (B) even when the violation is a matter of public record or is uncontested, there are substantial reasons that justify or mitigate the violation and make revocation inappropriate, and those reasons are complex or otherwise difficult to develop or present.

(e) Admissions by the Probationer. Before accepting an admission by a probationer that the probationer has violated a condition of probation or a lawful instruction issued by the supervising officer, the court shall determine that the probationer understands the following:

153

(1) the nature of the violation to which an admission is offered;

(2) the right to be represented by counsel as provided by Rule 27.3(d);

(3) the right to testify and to present witnesses and other evidence on the probationer's own behalf and to cross-examine adverse witnesses under subsection (f)(1); and

(4) that, if the alleged violation involves a criminal offense for which the probationer has not yet been tried, the probationer may still be tried for that offense and, although the probationer may not be required to testify, that any statement made by the probationer at the present proceeding may be used against the probationer at a subsequent proceeding or trial.

The court shall also determine that the probationer waives these rights, that the admission is voluntary and not the result of force, threats, coercion, or promises, and that there is a factual basis for the admission.

(f) Nature of the Hearing.
(1) The judge must find by a preponderance of the evidence that a violation of the conditions of probation or the instructions occurred. Each party shall have the right to present evidence and the right to confront and cross-examine adverse witnesses who appear and testify in person. The court may receive any reliable, relevant evidence not legally privileged, including hearsay.

(2) If the alleged violation involves a criminal offense for which the probationer has not yet been tried, the probationer shall be advised at the beginning of the revocation hearing that, regardless of the outcome of the revocation hearing, the probationer may still be held for that offense and that any statement made by the probationer at the hearing may be used against the probationer at a subsequent proceeding or trial.

(3) In cases involving breach of a condition of probation because of nonpayment of a fine, restitution, or court costs, incarceration shall not automatically follow nonpayment. Incarceration may be employed only after the court has examined the reasons for nonpayment and finds, on the record, that the probationer could have satisfied payment but refused to do so.

(g) Disposition. If the judge finds that a violation of the conditions of probation or lawful instructions occurred, it may revoke, modify, or continue probation.

(h) Record. The judge shall make a written statement or state for the record the evidence relied upon, and the reasons for, revoking probation.

Comment

Rule 27.3 is drafted to comply with the constitutional requirements articulated in *Gagnon v. Scarpelli*, 411 U.S. 778, 93 S. Ct. 1756, 36 L. Ed. 656 (1973). Rules 27.2 and 27.3 together set up a two-hearing process specifically required by *Gagnon*. Rule 27.2 provides for an informal preliminary hearing as prescribed by statute. Rule 27.3(a) then provides for the revocation hearing itself, as prescribed by statute. *See, e.g.,* Miss. Code Ann. § 47-7-37. *But see* Miss. Code Ann. §§ 47-7-38 (authorizes the Mississippi Department of Corrections "to impose graduated sanctions as an alternative to judicial modification or revocation" in certain instances), 47-7-38.1 (directs the Mississippi Department of Corrections to establish "technical violation centers" to detain probation violators for "technical violations").

Section (b) allows the probationer to waive a revocation hearing within carefully defined limits. Two hearings are not necessary if, at the first hearing, the probationer has received sufficient notice of the charges and of the evidence of the probation violation, and the probationer admits commission of the alleged violation consistent with section (e).

Section (d)(1) provides a probationer may be represented by retained counsel. Section (d)(2) states the right to appointed counsel for indigent probationers is determined on a case-by-case basis, through a due-process analysis. *See **Riely v. State***, 562 So. 2d 1206 (Miss. 1990); ***Gagnon***, 411 U.S. at 790-91.

The procedure for accepting an admission under section (e) applies at either the informal preliminary hearing or the revocation hearing. If there is no admission, the hearing is conducted pursuant to section (f).

Section (f)(3) recognizes the constitutional limits on revocation of probation for non-payment. As the United States Supreme Court explained in ***Bearden v. Georgia***, 461 U.S. 660, 103 S. Ct. 2064, 76 L. Ed. 2d 221 (1983):

> [I]n revocation proceedings for failure to pay a fine or restitution, a sentencing court must inquire into the reasons for the failure to pay. If the probationer willfully refused to pay or failed to make sufficient bona fide efforts legally to acquire the resources to pay, the court may revoke probation . . . . If the probationer could not pay despite sufficient bona fide efforts to acquire the resources to do so, the court must consider alternate measures of punishment other than imprisonment.

Id. at 672.

Section (h) is included to give a reviewing court a basis for evaluating the revocation hearing and decision. ***Gagnon*** requires that a written statement be made as to the evidence relied upon, and the reasons for, revoking probation. *See **Gagnon***, 411 U.S. at 786. A written judgment entry would constitute a sufficient written statement.

Rule 27.4 Other Proceedings.
Proceedings to revoke or modify any other suspended sentence or period of post-release supervision shall be conducted in accordance with Rule 27.

Comment
Rule 27.4 is consistent with existing statutes and case law. *See* Miss. Code Ann. §§ 47-7-34, 47-7-35, and 47-7-37 (post-release supervision);

Johnson v. State, 925 So. 2d 86 (Miss. 2006) (discussing imposition of suspended sentences).

Rule 28 Retention of Records and Evidence

The clerk of the court shall receive and maintain all papers, documents, and records filed, and all evidence admitted, in criminal cases. All records and evidence of the proceedings shall be retained according to law.

Comment

Rule 28 defines the basic duties of the clerk of court in criminal cases. On the retention of records as required by law, *see* Miss. Code Ann. § 9-7-128.

Rule 29 Appeals from Justice or Municipal Court

Rule 29.1 Notice of Appeal; Contents; Defects; Dismissal.
(a) Notice of Appeal. Any person adjudged guilty of a criminal offense by a justice or municipal court may appeal to county court or, if there is no county court, to circuit court, by filing simultaneously a written notice of appeal, and both a cost bond and an appearance bond (or cash deposit), as provided in Rules 29.3(a) and 29.4(a), with the clerk of the circuit court having jurisdiction within thirty (30) days of such judgment. This written notice of appeal and posting of the cost bond and the appearance bond (or cash deposit) perfects the appeal. After the filing of the written notice of appeal, cost bond, and appearance bond (or cash deposit), all further correspondence concerning the case shall be mailed directly to the circuit clerk for inclusion in the file.

(b) Contents. The written notice of appeal shall specify the party or parties taking the appeal; specify the current residence address and the current mailing address, if different, of each party taking the appeal; designate the judgment or order from which the appeal is taken; be addressed to county or circuit court, whichever appropriate; and state that the appeal is taken for a trial *de novo*.

(c) Defects in the Notice of Appeal; Dismissal. Upon a failure of a party to comply with the requirements of this rule as to content of the written notice of appeal, the court, on its own motion or on motion of a party, shall direct the clerk of the court to give written notice to the party in default, apprising the party of the nature of the deficiency. If the party in default fails to correct the deficiency within fourteen (14) days after notification, the appeal shall be dismissed by the clerk of the court. The county or circuit court shall promptly notify the lower court of any such dismissal.

Comment

Rule 29.1 incorporates provisions from former Rule 12.02(A.) of the Uniform Rules of Circuit and County Court.

Section (a) requires the notice of appeal to be filed with the clerk of the circuit court within thirty (30) days of entry of the judgment appealed from. *See Murray v. State*, 870 So. 2d 1182, 1184 (Miss. 2004) (holding the thirty (30) day deadline in procedural rule governs over conflicting statute). Under section (a), and unlike Rule 4(e) of the Mississippi Rules of Appellate Procedure, pending post-trial motions do not extend the time for taking an appeal; nor is the time for filing a notice of appeal extended if the lower court judge stays execution of the judgment. Section (c) requires that the lower court be promptly notified of any dismissal, so that execution of its judgment may proceed.

Rule 29.2 Record.

Upon receiving written notice of appeal, and upon the defendant's compliance with Rules 29.3(a) and 29.4(a), the circuit clerk shall promptly notify the lower court and the appropriate prosecuting attorney. Within ten (10) days after receipt of such notice, the judge or clerk of the lower court shall deliver to the clerk of the circuit court a certified copy of the record and all original papers in the case.

Comment

Rule 29.2 is consistent with former Rule 12.02(A.)(3.) of the Uniform Rules of Circuit and County Court.

Rule 29.3 Cost Bonds.

(a) Cost Bonds. Unless excused by the county or circuit court by the making of an affidavit of poverty like that specified in Mississippi Code Section 99-35-7, every defendant who appeals under this rule shall post a cash deposit, or bond with sufficient resident sureties (or licensed guaranty companies) to be approved by the circuit clerk, for all estimated court costs incurred both in the appellate and lower courts (including, but not limited to, fees, court costs, and amounts imposed pursuant to statute). The amount of such cash deposit or bond shall be determined by the judge of the lower court, payable to the State in an amount of not less than One Hundred Dollars ($100.00) nor more than Twenty-Five Hundred Dollars ($2,500.00). Upon a bond forfeiture, the costs of the lower court shall be recovered after the costs of the appellate court.

(b) Dismissal for Noncompliance. A defendant's failure to comply with Rule 29.3(a) shall be grounds for the court, on its own motion or on motion of a party, to dismiss the appeal, with costs. The county or circuit court shall promptly notify the lower court of any such dismissal.

Comment

Rule 29.3(a) is derived from former Rule 12.02(B.)(2.) of the Uniform Rules of Circuit and County Court. *See also* Miss. Code Ann. § 99-35-1 ("Any person appealing a judgment of a justice court or a municipal court under this section shall post bond for court costs relating to such appeal"). The purpose of the cost bond is to cover all estimated court costs, broadly defined, in both the trial and appellate court. Posting the cash deposit or bond stays execution of the judgment imposed by the lower court as it relates to fees, court costs, and amounts imposed pursuant to statute. Section (b) is taken directly from former Rule 12.02(A.)(1.) of the Uniform Rules of Circuit and County Court. Section (b) further provides that the lower court be promptly notified of the dismissal, so that execution of its judgment may proceed.

Rule 29.4 Appearance Bonds.

(a) Appearance Bond. Unless excused by the county or circuit court by the making of an affidavit as specified in Mississippi Code Section 99-35-7, a cash deposit, or bond with sufficient resident sureties (or licensed guaranty companies) to be approved by the circuit clerk, shall be given and conditioned on appearance before the county or circuit court from day to day and term to term until the appeal is finally determined or dismissed. The amount of such cash deposit or appearance bond shall be determined by the judge of the lower court.

(b) Failure to Appear. If the defendant fails to appear at the time and place set by the court, the court may dismiss the appeal with prejudice and with costs, and order forfeiture of the appearance bond or cash deposit. The county or circuit court shall promptly notify the lower court of any such dismissal.

(c) Time in Custody Credited. All time the defendant is in custody on the present charge shall be credited against any sentence imposed by the court.

Comment

Rule 29.4 continues the practice from former Rule 12.02(B.)(1.) and (3.) of the Uniform Rules of Circuit and County Court. The filing and approval of an appearance bond stays imposition of the sentence of incarceration. *See* Miss. Code Ann. § 99-35-3 (providing for appearance bonds).

Under section (c), a defendant's sentence includes credit for time already spent in custody on the present charge.

Rule 29.5 Proceedings.

Upon the filing with the circuit clerk of the written notice of appeal and bonds or cash deposits required by this Rule, unless excused therefrom, the prior judgment of conviction shall be stayed. The appeal shall proceed as a trial *de novo*. In appeals from justice or municipal court, when the maximum possible sentence is six (6) months or less, the case may be tried without a jury.

Comment

Rule 29.5 continues the practice from former Rule 12.02(C.) of the Uniform Rules of Circuit and County Court. *See also* Miss. Code Ann. § 99-35-1. As under Rule 18.1(a)(3), a jury trial is discretionary if a defendant's maximum possible sentence is six (6) months or less. *See **Hinton v. State***, 222 So. 2d 690, 692 (Miss. 1969).

Rule 30 Appeals from County Court

Rule 30.1 Notice of Appeal; Contents; Proceedings.
(a) Notice of Appeal. Any person adjudged guilty of a criminal offense by a county court, where the case was not a felony action transferred to that court from circuit court, may appeal to the circuit court having jurisdiction by filing written notice with the clerk of the circuit court within thirty (30) days of the entry of the final judgment. Extensions may be granted as provided in Mississippi Rule of Appellate Procedure 4(g).

(b) Contents. The notice of appeal shall specify the party or parties taking the appeal; designate the judgment or order from which the appeal is taken; state that the appeal is to circuit court; and state that the appeal is taken on the record. The clerk, upon receiving written notice of appeal, shall immediately send notice to the prosecuting attorney. Thereafter, appeals shall proceed as if in the Supreme Court and in accordance with the Mississippi Rules of Appellate Procedure.

(c) Proceedings. On appeal, legal arguments may be heard in any county within the jurisdiction of the circuit court and shall be considered solely on the record made in county court. If no prejudicial error be found, the circuit court shall affirm and enter judgment in like manner as affirmances in the Supreme Court. If prejudicial error be found, the circuit court shall reverse as is provided for reversals in the Supreme Court. If a new trial is granted, the cause shall be placed on the docket of the circuit court and a new trial held therein *de novo*.

Comment

Rule 30.1 largely continues practice under former Rules 12.03(A.), (C.), (D.), and (F.) of the Uniform Rules of Circuit and County Court. Essentially, a defendant may appeal a conviction in county court to the circuit court that has jurisdiction by filing a written notice of appeal with the clerk of the circuit court within thirty (30) days after entry of the final judgment (under former Rule 12.03(A.) of the Uniform Rules of Circuit and County Court, such written notice of appeal was filed with the clerk of the county court). *See* Miss. Code Ann. § 11-51-79. This includes cases that originated in county court and cases appealed to county court from justice or municipal court under Rule 29.1. Once the notice of appeal is filed, the case proceeds according to the Mississippi Rules of Appellate Procedure. Appeal of a conviction in circuit court is to the Mississippi Supreme Court, whether the case originated in county court, or in justice or municipal court. *See Jones v. City of Ridgeland*, 48 So. 3d 530 (Miss. 2009) (interpreting Miss. Code Ann. § 11-51-81).

As provided in Rule 30.3, Rule 30.1 does not apply to felony cases transferred by a circuit court to a county court for disposition. Nor does Rule 30.1 apply to a case assigned to a county court judge pursuant to Mississippi Code Section § 9-9-35, which remains throughout a circuit court case.

Rule 30.2 Bond.
Defendants who appeal a conviction in county court to circuit court shall be entitled to release pursuant to Rule 8.3. All time that the defendant has been in custody on the present charge shall be credited against any sentence imposed.

Comment
Rule 30.2 directs that Rule 8.3 governs release of defendants who appeal a conviction in county court to circuit court. As under prior Rule 12.03(B.) of the Uniform Rules of Circuit and County Court, a defendant is entitled to credit for time in custody on the present charge against any sentence imposed.

Rule 30.3 Felony Transfers.
Final judgments in felony cases transferred from circuit court to county court shall be appealed to the Supreme Court in the same manner as if the judgment were rendered in the circuit court.

Comment

Rule 30.3 follows practice under former Rule 12.03(E.) of the Uniform Rules of Circuit and County Court. *See also* Miss. Code Ann. §§ 9-9-27, 11-51-79.

Rule 31 Post-Conviction Collateral Relief

Applications for post-conviction collateral relief in criminal cases are governed by statute, as supplemented and modified by Rule 22 of the Mississippi Rules of Appellate Procedure.

Comment

Rule 31 confirms that applications for post-conviction collateral relief are governed by a comprehensive statutory process. *See* Miss. Code Ann. § 99-39-3(1).

Rule 32 Contempt

Rule 32.1 Applicability; Indirect and Direct Contempt Defined; Criminal and Civil Contempt Defined.

(a) Applicability. Rule 32 applies to both civil and criminal contempt arising in a criminal action.

(b) Indirect Contempt. "Indirect contempt," also known as "constructive contempt," means any contempt other than a direct contempt.

(c) Direct Contempt. "Direct contempt" means contempt committed:

(1) in the presence of the judge presiding in court; or

(2) so near to the judge as to interrupt the court's proceedings.

(d) Criminal Contempt. "Criminal contempt" means either:

(1) misconduct of a person that obstructs the administration of justice and that is committed either in the presence of the judge presiding in court or so near thereto as to interrupt its proceedings;

(2) willful disobedience or resistance of any person to a court's lawful writ, subpoena, process, order, rule, or command, where the primary purpose of the finding of contempt is to punish the contemnor; or

(3) any other willfully contumacious conduct which obstructs the administration of justice, or which lessens the dignity and authority of the court.

(e) Civil Contempt. "Civil contempt" means willful, continuing failure or refusal of any person to comply with a court's lawful writ, subpoena, process, order, rule or command that by its nature is still capable of being complied therewith.

Comment

Section (a) provides that Rule 32 applies both to civil and criminal contempt proceedings, so long as they arise out of a criminal case. *See* Rule 1.1.

The distinction between indirect (or constructive) contempt, defined by section (b), and direct contempt, defined by section (c), is drawn as a basis for procedural differences in applying a remedy. In those limited cases of direct contempt, where the contempt is within the judge's actual sight or hearing so that further or extrinsic evidence is not needed to show the judge what in fact occurred, the judge may dispose of the matter summarily under Rule 32.2. In all other instances the contempt is "indirect," which implicates additional procedural due process safeguards, such as specification of charges, notice, and a hearing. *See* Rules 32.3 through 32.5. *See In re Smith*, 926 So. 2d 878, 888 (Miss. 2006); *Cooper Tire & Rubber Co. v. McGill*, 890 So. 2d 859, 868-69 (Miss. 2004) (addressing "procedural safeguards" in cases of "constructive criminal contempt"); *Purvis v. Purvis*, 657 So. 2d 794, 798 (Miss. 1994).

The general distinction between criminal contempt, defined by section (d), and civil contempt, defined by section (e), is the purpose for which the sanctions are imposed, although the ultimate sanction in either case is incarceration. *See McGill*, 890 So. 2d at 867-68 ("[i]n classifying a finding of contempt as civil or criminal, this Court focuses on the *purpose* for which the power was exercised. . . . [T]he determination should focus on the character of the sanction itself and not the intent of the court imposing the sanction"). Where the sanction operates prospectively to ensure compliance with a lawful order of the court, the contempt is civil. *See Gutierrez v. Gutierrez*, 153 So. 3d 703, 712 (Miss. 2014) (citing *Jones v. Hargrove*, 516 So. 2d 1354, 1357 (Miss. 1987)) ("[t]he purpose of civil contempt is to compel parties to obey the orders of the court"); *Gaiennie v. McMillin*, 138 So. 3d 131, 136 (Miss. 2014) (quoting *Lahmann v. Hallmon*, 722 So. 2d 614, 620 (Miss. 1998)) ("The purpose of civil contempt is to enforce or coerce obedience to the orders of the court"); *Mingo v. State*, 944 So. 2d 18, 32 (Miss. 2006) (quoting *In re Williamson*, 838 So. 2d 226, 237 (Miss. 2002)) ("If the primary purpose of the contempt order is to enforce the rights of private party litigants or enforce compliance with a court order, then the contempt is civil"); *In re Smith*, 926 So. 2d at 887. The person being punished holds the keys to the jail and can purge himself/herself of contempt and gain release at any time by complying with the order. *See In re Smith*, 926 So. 2d at 887 (quoting *McGill*, 890 So. 2d at 868) ("The contemnor may be jailed or fined for civil contempt; however, the contemnor must be relieved of the penalty when he performs the required act"); *Jones*, 516 So. 2d at 1357; *Shillitani v. United States*, 384 U.S. 364, 86 S. Ct. 1531, 16 L. Ed. 2d 622 (1966); *Gompers v. Buck's Stove & Range Co.*, 221 U.S. 418, 31 S. Ct. 492, 55 L. Ed. 797 (1911). On the other hand, a criminal contempt proceeding is intended to punish for past, not contemplated or ongoing, conduct. *See Mingo*, 944 So. 2d at 32 (quoting *In re Williamson*, 838 So. 2d at 237) ("Criminal contempt penalties . . . are designed to punish the contemnor for disobedience of a court order; punishment is for past offenses and does not terminate upon compliance with the court order"); *In re Smith*, 926 So. 2d at 887-88. Its purpose is to vindicate the dignity of the court. Criminal contempt is a criminal offense for which a specific punishment is meted out, over which the defendant has no control. *See In re Smith*, 926 So. 2d at 887; *McGill*, 890 So. 2d at 868; *United States v. Barnett*, 376 U.S. 681, 84 S. Ct. 984, 12 L. Ed. 2d 23 (1964). If the conduct is extreme, contempt can be a serious crime entitling a defendant to certain constitutional safeguards (e.g., jury trial). *See* Miss. Code Ann. § 11-51-11(4); ***Bloom v. Illinois***, 391 U.S. 194, 88 S. Ct. 1477, 20 L. Ed. 2d 522 (1968).

Rule 32.2 Direct Contempt.
(a) Summary Imposition of Sanctions. The court against which a direct civil or criminal contempt has been committed may summarily impose sanctions on the person who committed it if:

> (1) the presiding judge has personally perceived the conduct constituting the contempt and has personal knowledge of the identity of the person committing it;

> (2) the contempt has interrupted the order of the court or interfered with the dignified conduct of the court's business; and

> (3) the punishment imposed does not exceed thirty (30) days incarceration or a fine of One-Hundred Dollars ($100.00).

The court shall afford the alleged contemnor an opportunity, consistent with the circumstances then existing, to present exculpatory or mitigating evidence. If the court summarily finds and announces on the record that direct contempt has been committed, the court may defer imposition or execution of sanctions until the conclusion of the proceeding during which the contempt was committed.

(b) Order of Contempt. Either before sanctions are imposed, or promptly thereafter, the court shall issue a written order stating, or shall state on the record, that a direct contempt has been committed and specifying:

> (1) whether the contempt is civil or criminal;

> (2) the evidentiary facts known to the court from the judge's own personal knowledge concerning the conduct constituting the contempt and, regarding any relevant evidentiary facts not so known, the basis of the court's findings;

(3) the sanction imposed for the contempt;

(4) in the case of civil contempt, how the contempt may be purged; and

(5) in the case of criminal contempt, if the sanction is incarceration, a determinate term.

(c) Review and Record.
(1) Review. The contemnor may seek review by appeal or by writ of habeas corpus, if appropriate.

(2) Record. The appellate record in cases of direct contempt in which sanctions have been summarily imposed shall consist of:

(1) the order of contempt; and, if the proceeding during which the contempt occurred was recorded, a transcript of that part of the proceeding; and

(2) any evidence admitted in the proceeding.

(d) No Summary Imposition of Sanctions. In any proceeding involving a direct contempt for which the court determines not to impose sanctions summarily, the judge shall issue a written order specifying the evidentiary facts within the personal knowledge of the judge respecting the conduct constituting the contempt and the identity of the contemnor. Thereafter, the proceeding shall be conducted pursuant to Rule 32.3 or Rule 32.4, whichever is applicable, and Rule 32.5 in the same manner as an indirect contempt.

Comment

Under section (a), sanctions may be imposed immediately upon a finding of direct contempt or deferred to the conclusion of the proceeding. A delay between citation for contempt and the imposition of sanctions can provide a cooling-off period in the relations between the judge and the contemnor, and is particularly relevant in those circumstances when the contemnor is a lawyer representing a client on trial. Delay gives all parties a chance to reacquire their objectivity, and also allows the contemnor time to discuss the matter with an attorney and prepare a statement. Deferral of a sanction does not, however, affect its summary nature. The sanction remains summary in nature in that no hearing is required; the court simply announces and imposes the sanction at the conclusion of the proceeding. By limiting the use of summary disposition to those cases where the alleged contemptuous conduct was committed in the presence of the judge, subsection (a)(1) recognizes that the judge can determine the facts surrounding an allegation of contempt without a hearing only when the judge personally witnesses the contemptuous conduct. As to possible constitutional limitations on the summary imposition of sanctions, including the right to jury trial and the right to counsel, *see, e.g.,* ***Taylor v. Hayes***, 418 U.S. 488, 94 S. Ct. 2697, 41 L. Ed. 2d 897 (1974); ***Codispoti v. Pennsylvania***, 418 U.S. 506, 94 S. Ct. 2687, 41 L. Ed. 2d 912 (1974); and ***Bloom v. Illinois***, 391 U.S. 194, 88 S. Ct. 1477, 20 L. Ed. 2d 522 (1968). Because of these limitations, summary procedures are available only when necessary to preserve order (subsection (a)(2)), and when the potential punishment does not exceed thirty (30) days incarceration or a One-Hundred Dollar ($100.00) fine (subsection (a)(3)). *See* Miss. Code Ann. § 9-1-17.

Section (a) does provide the contemnor with significant procedural rights, by requiring the court to "fin[d] and announc[e] on the record that direct contempt has been committed," and permitting the contemnor, "consistent with the circumstances then existing, to present exculpatory or mitigating evidence." Thus, the contemnor must be given notice of the charges and an opportunity to present information in mitigation of punishment. It should be recognized that the power to punish summarily for contempt is to be used cautiously, and is not an appropriate device to control every act of courtroom disrespect.

Section (c) establishes methods of review for direct contempts when sanctions are imposed summarily. *See, e.g.,* M.R.A.P. 21; Miss. Code Ann. §§ 11-51-11 (criminal contempt judgments), 11-51-12 (civil contempt judgments).

Section (d) limits the applicability of Rule 32.2 to direct contempts where sanctions are summarily imposed. Otherwise, the judge is required to issue a written order specifying the facts known to the judge to constitute the contempt, and the matter proceeds in the manner provided for indirect contempts under Rules 32.3 through 32.5.

Rule 32.3 Indirect Criminal Contempt; Commencement; Prosecution.
(a) Nature of the Proceedings. All criminal contempts not adjudicated pursuant to Rule 32.2 shall be prosecuted by means of a written motion or on the court's own initiative.

(b) Disqualification of the Judge. Indirect criminal contempt charges shall be heard by a judge other than the trial judge.

Comment

Section (a) provides that criminal contempts that are not, or cannot be, tried summarily in accordance with Rule 32.2 must be tried pursuant to the provisions of Rule 32.3, i.e., under the procedures established by these Rules for the trial of other criminal offenses. *See **Dennis v. Dennis***, 824 So. 2d 604, 609 (Miss. 2002) ("A defendant in [indirect] contempt proceedings is entitled to notice and is entitled to be informed of the nature and cause of the accusation, of his rights to be heard, to counsel, to call witnesses, to an unbiased judge, to a jury trial, and against self-incrimination, and that he is presumed innocent until proven guilty beyond reasonable doubt."). Section (a) requires contempt proceedings to be prosecuted by written motion or on the court's own initiative.

Section (b) requires that a new judge hold a hearing to determine the guilt of the contemnor, as well as to impose punishment, whenever the nature of the contemptuous conduct involves indirect criminal contempt. *See **Mississippi Comm'n on Jud. Performance v. Harris***, 131 So. 3d 1137, 1142 n.6 (Miss. 2013); ***Corr v. State***, 97 So. 3d 1211, 1216 (Miss. 2012). *But see **Purvis v. Purvis***, 657 So. 2d 794, 798 (Miss. 1994) (citing ***Mayberry v. Pennsylvania***, 400 U.S. 455, 463-64, 91 S. Ct. 499, 504, 27 L. Ed. 2d 532 (1971)) ("[d]irect contempt may be handled by the sitting judge instantly, although it is wise for a judge faced with personal attacks who waits till the end of the proceedings to have another judge take his place").

Rule 32.4 Indirect Civil Contempt.
(a) Commencement. A civil contempt proceeding may be commenced by the filing of a motion for contempt with the clerk of the court whose order or judgment is claimed to have been violated. No filing fee shall be required in connection with the filing of the motion for civil contempt. The proceeding shall be considered part of the action out of which the contempt arose.

(b) Contents of the Motion. The motion for civil contempt shall contain:

(1) a statement of the order or judgment involved, or a copy thereof, if available, and the name of the issuing judge where appropriate;

(2) the case caption and the docket number of the case;

(3) a short, concise statement of the facts on which the asserted contempt is based; and

(4) a request for the issuance of a summons as specified below.

The motion for civil contempt shall be verified or supported by affidavits.

(c) Summons. The summons shall issue only on a judge's order and shall direct the parties to appear before the court at a date and time certain for the purpose(s) specifically stated therein of:

(1) scheduling a trial;

(2) considering whether and when the filing of an answer is necessary;

(3) considering whether discovery is necessary;

(4) holding a hearing on the merits of the motion; or

(5) considering such other matters or performing such other acts as the court may deem appropriate.

A hearing on the merits of the motion shall be held not less than seven (7) days after service of the summons.

(d) Service of the Summons and Motion. The following shall be served upon the alleged contemnor:

(1) a copy of the summons;

(2) a copy of the motion for civil contempt;

(3) a copy of the accompanying affidavits; and

(4) if incarceration to compel compliance is sought, notice to the alleged contemnor in the following form:

TO THE PERSON ALLEGED TO BE IN CONTEMPT OF COURT:

1. It is alleged that you have disobeyed a court order, are in contempt of court, and should go to jail until you obey the court's order.

2. You have the right to have a lawyer. If you already have a lawyer, you should consult the lawyer at once. If you do not now have a lawyer, please note:

(a) A lawyer can be helpful to you by:

(1) explaining the allegations against you;

(2) helping you determine and present any defense to those allegations;

(3) explaining to you the possible outcomes; and

(4) helping you at the hearing.

(b) Even if you do not plan to contest that you are in contempt of court, a lawyer can be helpful.

(c) If you want a lawyer but do not have the money to hire one, you may ask the court to appoint one for you.

3. IF YOU DO NOT APPEAR FOR A SCHEDULED COURT HEARING BEFORE THE JUDGE, YOU WILL BE SUBJECT TO ARREST.

Comment

Rule 32.4 applies to all proceedings to enforce compliance with orders or judgments formalized by court order, for the violation of which civil contempt is an appropriate remedy. Section (a) provides that indirect civil contempt proceedings are initiated by motion and clarifies that they are treated as part of the action out of which the contempt arose. Consequently, no filing fee is required.

Section (b) prescribes what must be included in an indirect civil contempt motion and, because of the serious nature of an allegation of civil contempt, requires verification or accompanying appropriate affidavits.

Section (c) endows the summons with unusual significance. Because of the expedited and grave nature of a civil contempt proceeding, the summons: "issue[s] only on a judge's order"; must "direct the parties to appear before the court at a date and time certain" after service of the order; and must specifically state what will happen when the parties appear. Section (c) seeks to permit flexibility with respect to what occurs when the parties first appear in answer to the summons. Depending on the nature of the alleged contempt, a case may or may not benefit from the filing of an answer, expedited discovery, or an immediate hearing. Consequently, the rule gives wide discretion to the judge to determine what should happen when the parties appear: a "hearing on the merits," if it makes sense to have that quickly; scheduling a trial; considering dispensing with an answer; expediting discovery, if discovery is necessary; requiring initial compliance by the defendant pending a hearing; or considering other appropriate matters or requiring other appropriate acts to be performed. Under section (c)(3), a party must seek an order permitting discovery, unlike normal discovery provisions which permit parties, on their own, to initiate discovery.

Rule 32.5 Further Proceedings.
(a) Consolidation of Criminal and Civil Contempts. If a person has been charged with more than one (1) contempt pursuant to Rule 32.3, Rule 32.4, or both, the court may consolidate the proceedings for hearing and disposition.

(b) When Judge Disqualified. A judge who enters an order pursuant to Rule 32.2(d), institutes an indirect contempt proceeding on the court's own initiative pursuant to Rule 32.3 or Rule 32.4, or reasonably expects to be called as a witness at any hearing on the matter, is disqualified from sitting at the hearing.

(c) Failure to Appear at Hearing.
(1) Generally. If, after proper notice, the alleged contemnor fails to appear personally at the time and place set by the court, the court may enter an order directing the alleged contemnor be taken into custody and brought before the court or judge designated in the order.

(2) Civil Contempt. If, after proper notice, the alleged contemnor in a civil contempt proceeding fails to appear in person or by counsel at the time and place set by the court, the court may proceed in the alleged contemnor's absence.

(d) Disposition. When a court makes a finding of contempt, the court shall issue a written order that specifies the sanction imposed for the contempt. In the case of a civil contempt, the order shall specify how the contempt may be purged. In the case of a criminal contempt, if the sanction is incarceration, the order shall specify a determinate term.

Rule 32.6 Bail. A contemnor incarcerated for contempt is entitled to the same consideration with respect to bail pending appeal as a defendant convicted in a criminal proceeding, as provided by law.

Comment

Rule 8.3 generally provides that "[a] convicted defendant shall be entitled to bail pending appeal as prescribed by Mississippi Code Section 99-35-115." But Mississippi Code Sections 11-51-11 and 11-51-12 specifically address bond in appeals from criminal and civil contempt judgments. *See* Miss. Code Ann. §§ 11-51-11, 11-51-12.

Rule 33 Subpoenas

(a) Generally. Except as set forth below, the procedures for subpoenas shall conform to Rule 45 of the Mississippi Rules of Civil Procedure. This Rule shall not apply to proceedings before a grand jury.

(b) Subpoenas *Duces Tecum* for Production at Trial or Hearing. A subpoena may, without a motion or hearing, require the production of books, papers, documents or other objects at the date, time and place at which the trial, hearing or proceeding at which these items are to be offered in evidence is scheduled to take place.

(c) Subpoenas *Duces Tecum* for Production other than at Trial or Hearing.
(1) Generally. No subpoena may require the production of books, papers, documents or other objects at a date and time or place other than the date, time and place at which the trial, hearing or proceeding at which these items are to be offered in evidence is scheduled to take place, unless the court has entered an order pursuant to this Rule authorizing the issuance of such subpoena.

(2) Motions; Service; Opposition. A hearing on a motion for the issuance of a subpoena *duces tecum* shall be set at the time the motion is filed and served. The hearing shall be set no earlier than ten (10) days after filing and service of the motion. Except for good cause shown, all motions for subpoenas *duces tecum* shall be served on:

(A) the custodian of the books, papers, documents or other objects which would be subject to the subpoena;

(B) all parties;

(C) all persons whose books, papers, documents or other objects would be subject to the subpoena; and

(D) all persons who may have a claim that privileged material would be subject to the subpoena.

Any party to the action or other interested person may file an opposition or response.

(3) Supporting Affidavit or Declaration. Motions seeking subpoenas *duces tecum* shall be supported by an affidavit or declaration stating facts which establish:

(A) the documents or objects sought are evidentiary and relevant;

(B) the documents or objects sought are not otherwise reasonably procurable in advance of the trial, hearing or proceeding by exercise of due diligence;

(C) the moving party cannot properly prepare for trial without such production and inspection in advance of trial and the failure to obtain such inspection may tend unreasonably to delay the trial; and

(D) the application is made in good faith and is not intended for the purpose of general discovery.

(4) Immediate Lodging with Court. Any subpoena *duces tecum* under section (c) shall be returnable to, and the items sought thereunder produced before, the court. In the event that materials subject to a subpoena are received by a party, an attorney, or an attorney's agent or investigator directly from the subpoenaed

person, any person receiving such materials shall immediately notify the court and shall immediately lodge such materials with the court. The materials shall not be opened, reviewed or copied by a recipient without a prior court order.

(d) Sanctions. Violation of this Rule may provide a basis for sanctions.

Comment

Rule 33 is derived from former Rule 2.01 of the Uniform Rules of Circuit and County Court.

Rule 34 Motions

Rule 34.1 Motions: Form, Content, Rights of Reply.
(a) In General. A party applying to the court for an order must do so by motion.

(b) Form and Content of a Motion. A motion – except when made during a trial or hearing – must be in writing, unless the court permits the party to make the motion by other means. A motion shall contain a concise statement of the precise relief requested and shall state the specific factual grounds and specific legal authority in support thereof. A motion may be supported by affidavit. The requirement of writing is fulfilled if the motion is stated in a written notice of the hearing of the motion or if the matter is presented in an agreed order.

(c) Rights of Reply. Unless otherwise ordered by the court, each party may file and serve a response within ten (10) days after service of the motion, and the moving party may file and serve a reply, which shall be directed only to matters raised in a response, within five (5) days after service of the response. Responses and replies shall be in the form required for motions.

Comment

Rule 34 is consistent with common practice as embodied in Rule 47 of the Federal Rules of Criminal Procedure, Rule 7(b) of the Mississippi Rules of Civil Procedure, and former Rule 6.07 of the Uniform Rules of Circuit and County

Court. Rule 34.1 is intended to provide general standards governing the details of motion practice in criminal cases; the general standards will, of course, be inapplicable when a Rule specifies a different procedure. Sections (a) and (b) are intended to produce concise, but precise pleadings. To this end, section (b) requires a statement of the "specific factual grounds" for the relief requested.

Section (b) eliminates the requirement of writing for motions made during a trial or hearing. The language "other means" in section (b) broadly permits the court to entertain motions through electronic or other reliable methods. The sentence in section (b) permitting a motion to be "supported by affidavit" is not intended to permit "speaking motions," but to authorize the use of affidavits when they are appropriate to establish a fact.

Unless otherwise ordered by the court, section (c) provides a right (but not a duty) to respond to all motions. Permitting a reply by the moving party to the response to the motion allows the moving party an opportunity to address new issues that the opposing party may have raised in the response.

Rule 34.2 Hearing; Oral Argument.

Upon request of any party, or on its own initiative, the court may set any motion for hearing. The court may limit or deny oral argument on any motion. It is the duty of the movant, when a motion or other pleading is filed (including a motion for a new trial), to pursue the motion to hearing and decision. Failure to pursue a pretrial motion to hearing and decision before trial is deemed an abandonment of that motion; however, the motion may be heard after the commencement of trial.

Comment

Rule 34.2 is based on former Rule 2.04 of the Uniform Rules of Circuit and County Court. The hearing and oral argument provisions are intended to give the court maximum discretion in deciding what procedures, in addition to the written motion and memoranda, will be most helpful to it in reaching a reasoned and expeditious decision on each issue. No party has an absolute right to oral argument on a motion.

Rule 34.3 Waiver of Formal Requirements.

Upon request of any party, or on its own initiative, the court may waive a requirement specified in this Rule or overlook a formal defect in a motion or request.

Comment

This inherent power of the court is specifically included for purposes of clarity, and to allow its exercise informally. Rule 34.3 should be used primarily to allow handwritten documents to be submitted by indigent defendants or persons without counsel; it should not be used to sanction deviations which affect an opposing party's substantial rights.

Rule 34.4 Service and Filing.

Unless otherwise specified in these Rules, the manner and sufficiency of service and filing of motions, requests, petitions, applications, and all other pleadings and documents shall be governed by Rule 1.7.

Rule 34.5 Entry of Order and Duty of Clerk.

Immediately upon entry of an order or judgment of the court, the clerk of court shall make a diligent effort to ensure that all attorneys of record have received notice of the entry of the order.

Comment

Rule 34.5 continues practice under former Rule 11.05 of the Uniform Rules of Circuit and County Court.

APPENDIX

SAMPLE CHARGE TO GRAND JURY

You have been summoned and sworn as a grand juror of the Circuit Court for _____ County (__ Judicial District) of the _____ Judicial Circuit of the State of Mississippi. As members of the Grand Jury, you are a part of the judicial branch of state government, an arm of this circuit court. The law of this state provides that grand juries are empaneled and charged concerning their duties only by the circuit judge. In compliance with this law, the court, before you begin your work, instructs you concerning your duties as members of the grand jury. It is mandatory that you follow these instructions and should you deem, during your service, need of additional instructions, you should present this request to the court. The law of this state specifies the express powers of grand juries. The grand jury has the power of indictment or presentment in a crime and the additional authority to issue reports.

The Grand Jury is an ancient and honored institution. Its existence is firmly imbedded in the system of Anglo-Saxon justice which we inherited from England. It is guaranteed in the constitution, which provides that no person may be placed on trial for a felony unless he or she has been indicted by a grand jury. This provision stands as a barrier against unjust prosecution by persons in authority. The grand jury is the means, not only of bringing to trial persons accused of crime, but also to protect persons from unfounded accusations whether presented by legal officers or by others who may be motivated by public clamor or private malice. Your duty is to allow or to deny issuance of an indictment. There are from 15 to 25 members of a grand jury and 12 members must agree before you can approve an indictment. The words "true bill" are used to indicate an indictment that you have approved. Each indictment must be signed by the foreman and may be signed by one of the prosecuting attorneys.

You will hear only one side of a case. It is not your duty to decide the guilt or innocence of the accused. It is your duty to determine whether there is sufficient evidence or probable cause to require an accused to stand trial. If the evidence establishes a probability that a crime was committed and that the defendant committed the crime, then you should return a "true bill." If you do not have an indictment before the grand jury, you may return a presentment, which is an instruction for an indictment to be drawn. If the evidence fails to establish a probability that a crime was committed and that the defendant is guilty of that crime, then you must refuse to return a "true bill." You should prepare a list of the cases upon which you have refused to return a "true bill" and return that list to the court.

No public purpose would be served by indicting a person when it appears to you that the evidence is not sufficient to sustain a conviction. Unjust or unfounded indictments should not be returned against anyone. On the other hand, it is equally important that indictments be returned against those who, upon the evidence, appear to be probably guilty of the commission of a crime. Anyone you indict shall receive a speedy public trial to determine their guilt or innocence.

You must be fair and just in your deliberations to the best of your ability and understanding. Your oath requires that you do not indict any person through malice, hatred or ill will; nor will you fail to indict any person through fear, favor, regard, reward, or hope of reward. You must be guided by an impartial spirit free from personal, social, racial, religious or political bias or feeling.

You are cautioned that rumor and hearsay testimony are unreliable. Also, that no person may be compelled to be a witness against himself/herself. A witness who testifies about his/her own participation in a crime must first be advised in your presence of his/her constitutional rights by the prosecuting attorney(s) before you may accept such evidence. You determine what witnesses you will permit to appear and testify before you.

The district attorney, county attorney and attorney general are by law the representatives of the State of Mississippi in all criminal prosecutions. It is the duty of the district attorney and county attorney to be present with the grand jury in the room to present the evidence, to examine the witnesses and to give advice on any matter of law which may be raised. You are entitled to the legal advice of the prosecuting attorney(s) on matters of law unless you are instructed to the contrary by the court. You are, however, the sole judges of the facts and the prosecuting attorney(s) may not influence you as to whether an indictment will be approved. After the testimony is taken and you are discussing what action you will take, the prosecuting attorney(s) will withdraw from your jury room. They are not permitted to be present during your deliberations nor when a ballot is taken and they may not influence your decision on any question of fact. You may request the advice and assistance of the attorney general of the state. You are also at liberty at any time to call for further instructions from the court, although the instruction which the prosecuting attorney(s) give you will usually be sufficient.

You are an independent body. You, as well as the prosecuting attorney(s), have the right to require the clerk of this court to issue subpoenas for witnesses to be brought before you to testify. Your foreman shall keep a record of the names of all witnesses sworn before the grand jury. This list of witnesses, certified and signed by the foreman, shall be returned to the court.

The grand jury has the important duty of making certain mandatory investigations and inspections. The grand jury must:

1. You must make a personal inspection of the county jail, its condition, sufficiency for the safekeeping of prisoners, and their accommodation and health, and make a report on the same to the court.

2. You must examine the tax collector's books and his/her reports and settlements, and make a report on the same to the court.

3. You must examine the status of forest protection in the county, and in doing so, you are charged in particular of the crimes of setting fires as set forth in § 95-5-25 and § 97-17-13 of the Mississippi Code of 1972.

In addition, you, the grand jury, may make additional investigations and make reports on the same on your own initiative. Thus, you may investigate how officials are conducting their public trust, and make investigations as to the proper conduct of public institutions. This gives you the power to inspect such institutions, and if you decide, to call before you those in charge of their operations, and such other persons who can testify in that regard. If, as a result of such an investigation, it is determined that an improper condition exists, you may recommend a remedy. You shall have free access at all proper hours to papers, records, accounts and books of all county officers, including written reports of prior grand juries, for all examinations which in your discretion you may see fit to make, and may report to the court in relation thereto. While you may indict any person, you should not accuse any person by name of an offense, malfeasance, or misfeasance unless an indictment is returned. It is not your duty or responsibility to make reports praising performance of public duty by certain or all public officials. This is their duty under the law and their oath of office requires their diligent performance of lawful duties, and any such report by you could serve no purpose other than that of partisan politics.

The law requires that the circuit court shall charge you particularly concerning enforcement of the following laws:

1. Those against unlawful gambling and handling of intoxicating liquors;

2. Those relating to gambling with minors and the giving or selling to them tobacco, narcotics, or liquors;

3. Those providing for the assessment, collection and disbursement of the public revenues, state and county;

4. Those defining the duties of public officers;

5. Those relating to the collection and paying over of fines and forfeitures;

6. Those relating to providing fire escapes in hotels, theaters and other buildings;

7. Those relating to the management of 16th section school trust lands;

8. The law in relation to the illegal possession and sale of barbiturate acid and narcotics, and all other substances under the Controlled Substances Act, § 49-29-101 and following sections;

9. Section 47-1-31, prisoners, records, treatment and condition;

10. Section 47-1-27, responsibility of custodian of county prisoners;

11. Section 45-11-1, fire protection and safety;

12. Schools;

13. Motels, hotels, lodging houses, public buildings;

14. Handling of juveniles (In Harrison County only - The purposes and provisions of Chapter 23 of Title 43, "Family Court.");

15. Ambulance service;

16. Pollution of streams;

17. Hospitals;

18. Nursing homes;

19. Elections, corrupt practices, Section 23-3-27, *et seq.*;

20. The condition of the county roads and the performance of the duties of contractors, overseers and supervisors under § 65-7-119; and

21. Such other statutes as the circuit judge deems proper.

The oath which you have taken contains essential principles which govern you in your deliberations. The oath is your promise that you will keep secret what takes place in the grand jury room. A grand juror, except when called as a witness in court, shall not disclose any proceedings or action in relation to offenses brought before it for six months after the adjournment of the grand jury upon which the juror served. A grand juror shall not disclose the name or testimony of any witness who has been before the grand jury. Any disclosure of secrets within the six month period is punishable by fine or imprisonment for contempt of court.

The purpose of the secrecy requirement is two-fold:

1.   Accusations may be brought before you which you find unfounded. If publicity were given to the fact that the grand jury investigated a person, that person's reputation might be ruined even though the person is entirely innocent; and

2.   If anyone charged with a crime learns of your investigation, that person would be given an opportunity to escape and defeat the process of criminal justice.

This requirement of secrecy demands that you do not communicate to anyone what has been said or done in the grand jury room unless you are ordered by a judge in open court to reveal it. You should report any person asking you, or attempting to ask you, what has occurred in the grand jury room. It does not matter if the attempt was in person, by phone, letter or otherwise; you should report such a question or attempt to the court and to the prosecuting attorney(s).

I want to thank each one of you for taking time out of your busy lives to perform this important civic duty. You are making a personal sacrifice, but I believe you will find this experience one of the most interesting in your lives. Furthermore, at the end of your service, you will have the satisfaction of having helped render justice among your neighbors.